ANTHROPOLOGICAL PAPERS

OF THE

American Museum of Natural History.

VOL. V, PART I.

MATERIAL CULTURE OF THE BLACKFOOT INDIANS.

BY CLARK WISSLER.

NEW YORK:
Published by Order of the Trustees.
1910.

Library of Congress Cataloging in Publication Data

Wissler, Clark, 1870-1947.
    Material culture of the Blackfoot Indians.

    Reprint of the 1910 ed. published by order of the
Trustees of the American Museum of Natural History,
New York, which was issued as v. 5, pt. 1 of the Museum's
Anthropological papers.
    Bibliography: p.
    1. Siksika Indians. I. Title. II. Series: American
Museum of Natural History, New York. Anthropological
papers; v. 5.
E99.S54W52   1975   971.2'004'97   74-9018
ISBN 0-404-11915-8

Reprinted from the edition of 1910, New York
First AMS edition published in 1975
Manufactured in the United States of America

AMS PRESS INC.
NEW YORK, N. Y. 10003

CORRECTIONS.

ANTHROPOLOGICAL PAPERS

OF THE

AMERICAN MUSEUM OF NATURAL HISTORY

VOL. V, PART I.

MATERIAL CULTURE OF THE BLACKFOOT INDIANS.

BY CLARK WISSLER.

CONTENTS.

ILLUSTRATIONS.

PLATES.

TEXT FIGURES.

INTRODUCTION.

In this second paper of a series upon the Blackfoot Indians, the writer is again greatly indebted to Mr. D. C. Duvall, without whose aid and interest much of the information could not have been secured. As before, the greater part of the data come from the Piegan and Blood divisions, yet, many of our informants among these divisions were quite familiar with the life of the Northern Blackfoot, so that the statements given, may be taken as fairly representative. In rendering this characterization of Blackfoot material culture we have made use of such comparative data as came readily to hand, that this culture might be seen, not in isolation, but in relation to other cultures. Occasionally, we have carried these comparisons to considerable length in order to follow what seemed to be suggestions of former historical relations among the tribes concerned. In no case, however, have we sought to make a complete cultural survey of the Plains area. In the discussion we have followed the data gathered by us in the field but at the same time have taken note of the literature, especially that of the older writers, and in using the footnotes the reader should bear in mind that, unless the contrary is stated, the citations are given as confirmation and not as authority for the statements in the text. The works of greatest value to the student of the Blackfoot are the journal of the younger Henry, the writings of Maximilian and the later but much more complete accounts by George Bird Grinnell. As the first dates back to about 1808, the last to the years immediately preceding 1890, and our own data to some twenty years later, these taken together give us a view of Blackfoot cultural history spanning a century, or almost the entire period they are known to history. We have sought by the supplementary aid of all previous contributions to present a fairly complete view of this culture as it existed in its historic prime, recognizing, however, that at all times during this interval it was subject to modification from contact with both white and Indian, and that it can not be said to have been strictly stationary at any time during the period.

We have made frequent reference to the subject matter of myths and narratives published in Volume II of this series in which appear confirmations of our other data but also presentations of cultural habits in a functional setting of daily events, thus affording a more realistic view of Blackfoot life.

Acknowledgments are due Dr. Robert H. Lowie for important data from the Northern Blackfoot and to Mr. Walter McClintock for many suggestions both in the field and at home.   Recognition also should be given the many officials and traders of the various reservations and the Canadian mounted police, all of whom assisted us in many ways necessary to our success.   In the preparation of the manuscript Mr. William C. Orchard gave special assistance with the tipi ties and worked out many moccasin patterns and quill techniques found in the area, descriptions of which he contributed to the text as indicated therein.   Miss Ruth B. Howe made the drawings and contributed data on the types of stitches.   For assistance with the manuscript and proof, the writer is under obligations to Miss Bella Weitzner.

CLARK WISSLER.

New York.

October 1, 1909.

ETHNOGRAPHY.

As the aim of this paper is to present Blackfoot material culture in perspective rather than in isolation, some ethnographic discussion seems in order. Many older writers speak of a Blackfoot confederacy composed of the Blackfoot, Sarcee, and Gros Ventre. Occasionally, the Kootenai are included. We found no evidence of any bonds between these tribes other than the usual alternating periods of friendship and strife. Thus, while the Sarcee seem to have been regarded as in a sense near relatives, the Gros Ventre and Kootenai were often treated as enemies. The Flatheads, Nez Perce, Northern Shoshone, Crow, Haidatsa, Assiniboine and Cree were usually considered as enemies, though there were, as among Indians of this area, alternate periods of hostility and truce. In many narratives, we find the young men fall to fighting while their elders are discussing peace in council, which indicates, in a characteristic manner, the status of intertribal relations. It is true that within historical times there did exist a bond of blood due to intermarriage between the Blackfoot on one hand and the Sarcee and Gros Ventre on the other, but there is no evidence for the existence of a formal political alliance of any sort.

The Blackfoot call themselves Siksikauw^a (black-foot-people). In addition to the main body, there were two tribes: the Kainaw^a, or Blood, and the Pikunjiw^a, or Piegan. So far as could be learned, these divisions recognized no sovereignty of the main body, though all considered themselves bound by ties of common descent. For many years the main body, or Northern Blackfoot, together with the Blood and some Piegan, have lived on separate reservations in Alberta. The greater part of the Piegan occupy a reservation in Montana. In consequence of this location, the Piegan·are usually spoken of as the Northern and Southern Piegan respectively, who, if not now ethnically distinct, are at least politically so.

Mention of the Blackfoot will be found in most of the journals and narratives of the fur traders of the Old Northwest. From such of these as are available, it appears that in 1787, at least, the Blackfoot were already a typical Plains people, provided with horses and living chiefly upon the buffalo. The most precise definition of the country occupied by the Piegan is given by Henry, who says that they occupied in 1810 the same territory as when first met by traders.[1] This was along the foot of the Rocky Moun-

---

[1] Henry and Thompson, 670, 704.

tains on the head waters of the various branches of the Saskatchewan. Bow River is mentioned as their chief place of residence and Thompson reported several camps near the present site of Calgary. Henry also mentions their driving buffalo along Red Deer River, probably south and southeast of Rocky Mountain House. Throughout his journal, the Piegan are considered as near the mountains and he makes the interesting statement that one band lived almost entirely in the foothills, trapping beaver and seldom resorting to the Plains. The general import of Henry's account is that the home of the Piegan was in Alberta, along and south of the present main line of the Canadian Pacific Railroad. Mackenzie's [1] account is much the same, but more inclusive, for he says that they lived on the head waters of the south branch of the Saskatchewan, which area would comprise a large triangular portion of Alberta between the Belly and Bow Rivers. However, the probability is, that Mackenzie had only the Bow River in mind. Thompson, according to his editor's note, first named Bow River, Pekakemew or Pekahkemew.[2] This was evidently intended for Piegan.[3] Yet, the best proof that the Piegan lived near the mountains is that they traded at Rocky Mountain House, on Clearwater River, which post, according to Henry, was opened expressly for trade with the Piegan, Sarcee and Gros Ventre.[4] Curiously, Harmon does not mention the Piegan on his map, but places Gros Ventre between Red Deer and Bad Rivers.

The Blood and Blackfoot traded at the mouth of Vermillion River and at Fort Augustus (Edmonton) which would place them northeast of the Piegan.[5] All accounts agree in placing the Blood adjacent to the Piegan, and Mackenzie [6] states that they ranged on the south branch of the Saskatchewan. This would be along the Red Deer River and southward. Somewhere to the east or northeast of these were the Blackfoot.

The whole territory of the Piegan, Blood and Blackfoot is defined by Henry as follows:— "a line due south from Vermillion Fort to the south branch of the Saskatchewan and up that stream to the foot of the Rocky Mountains; then goes N. along the mountains until it strikes the N. branch of the Saskatchewan, and down that stream to Vermillion River." [7] Henry was remarkably exact in the location of trading posts, etc., from which it is reasonable to infer that he took pains to inform himself as to the boundaries of the Indians. Yet, he is not quite consistent as to the southern boundary,

---

[1] Mackenzie, lxx.

[2] Henry and Thompson, 485.

[3] Maclean, (h), 21, states that Bow River is named from the wood found on its banks suitable for making bows.

[4] Henry and Thompson, 721.

[5] Henry and Thompson, 506, 576.

[6] Mackenzie, lxx.

[7] Henry and Thompson, 524.

for in speaking of the Piegan in another place, he says that they extended to the Missouri.[1] That they sometimes went to that river is certain, but trading establishments were not opened upon that stream or in the adjacent parts of the valley until about 1831, which would of itself account for a tendency on the part of these tribes to camp on the Saskatchewan near the posts of Henry.

The Gros Ventre, Fall Indians, or Atsina, seem to have lived in the fork of the Bow River and Red Deer River. Umfreville, who seems to be the first to mention these people, is not very definite in his location of their territory but placed them on the south branch of the Saskatchewan from the rapids of which they took the name of Fall Indians. He claims that communication with them was by means of the Blackfoot language since many of them could speak that tongue. It is also interesting to note that while he found a great deal of intermarriage, the Blackfoot did not learn the language of the Gros Ventre.[2] Henry made a precise statement as to the home of the Gros Ventre to the effect that formerly they occupied the point of land between Red Deer and Bow Rivers but now (1810) reside south of the Piegan on the head waters of streams entering the Missouri.[3] This would place them within the present bounds and eastward of the Blackfoot Indian Reservation, Montana. The journal of Harmon makes frequent mention of the Fall Indians as residing on the South Branch between the Assiniboine and the Blackfoot. Hayden gives the most complete historical account, but, as to the sources of his information, the writer is ignorant. The general import of all our information is that at or about 1800 the Gros Ventre lived along the South Branch of the Saskatchewan and perhaps on the head waters of the Marias and Milk Rivers. They seem to have made journeys to the south and also to the east into the country of the Assiniboine with whom and with the Cree they were often at war.

We have yet to consider the Sarcee. Umfreville[4] speaks of them as seldom visiting his post and that they had recently fallen out with the Blood. Henry[5] devotes a paragraph to the Sarcee in which it is inferred that until about 1800 they lived on the north side of the north branch of the Saskatchewan, hunted beaver and made themselves useful to the fur traders, but that after that date they spent a great deal of time on the south side,

---

[1] Henry and Thompson, 723.
[2] Henry and Thompson, 485, note that the south branch of the Saskatchewan was sometimes called Big Belly Fork. The present Belly River in Alberta is noted by Maclean, (h) p. 21, as having received its name from the Gros Ventre who once lived in its valley. However, the modern Piegan claim that the name is their own and has no reference to the Gros Ventre.
[3] Henry and Thompson, 530.
[4] Umfreville, 198.
[5] Henry and Thompson, 532, 737.

where, with the Blackfoot, they feasted on buffalo. Their usual abode was about the Beaver Hills. The Sarcee are a tribe of the Beaver, or Castor Indians residing at that time on the Peace River. So far as known, these Beaver Indians did not possess the manners and customs of the Plains Indians, but in 1810 Henry says that the Sarcee were the same as "the other Meadow Indians." Harmon prepared a map showing the distribution of tribes in his time and, though this is a copy of Mackenzie's map, the editor claims that Harmon re-located the tribes. On this map, the Sarcee are placed next to the mountains to the northwest of Penbina River, partly separated from the Beaver Indians on Peace River by the western limits of the Cree. This would place them north of Rocky Mountain House. Maclean [1] gives a brief but interesting account of the Sarcee in which he recites traditional accounts of their separation from the main body to the effect, that, as a small band they seceded, going down to Lesser Slave Lake and to the Plains. They were lost to their kindred for more than a century and discovered by some visiting Beaver Indians at a trading post on the Saskatchewan. This writer claims them to be the oldest inhabitants of the Plains, though upon what ground is not stated. He discusses their probable number, quoting Sir John Franklin and other writers, and finds that the estimates vary from 300 to 1200 persons. They seem to have roamed a great deal; in 1843 they were found upon the Marias River. While they retained their native language, many of them spoke Cree and Blackfoot.[2]

The distribution of the group is now fairly defined in the period of 1784–1810. The Sarcee kept well toward the mountains above Rocky Mountain House and toward Edmonton, and the Piegan below Rocky Mountain House toward the head waters of the Milk and Marias Rivers. Touching the latter on the south and east, were the Gros Ventre. These three extended like a crescent over the head waters of the Saskatchewan. In the vicinity of Red Deer River were the Blood and beyond them toward Battle River were the Blackfoot. It is not to be inferred that these tribes rigidly respected these boundaries for they were disposed to the roving, hunting life of all Plains Indians and were much given to intertribal intercourse.

So far we have not given much consideration to the evidence for the southern boundary of Blackfoot territory. Lewis and Clark made their journey along the upper Missouri without meeting the Piegan or Gros Ventre, though they were in fear of the latter. On the return trip Lewis ascended the Marias and its northern branch, Cut Bank, to within about twenty miles of the foothills of the mountains, where his party found abandoned camps and later, on Two Medicine River, fell in with the Indians. Lewis

---

[1] Maclean, (i), 9–19.
[2] Henry and Thompson, 737.

claims to have asked them if they were Gros Ventre and to have received an affirmative answer. The editor of Lewis and Clark's journals has identified them as belonging to the Blackfoot, probably Piegan.[1] Grinnell, as quoted by Wheeler,[2] states that in 1895, a Piegan named Wolf Calf was living who claimed to have been a member of this party of Indians. We have heard the details of this from Piegan now living and find the narratives not only consistent with themselves, but with the account of Lewis. Scott argues that the Indians met by Lewis were not Blackfoot.[3] His evidence is that the spot where the engagement occurred was Gros Ventre territory, and Lewis' statement of identification. The former counts for nothing in this case, and as to the latter, an examination of Lewis' journal indicates a tendency to use the term Gros Ventre of the Prairies for the whole area of Northern Montana and upward. Further, as he was expecting to fall in with this tribe his identification should not be given absolute validity. We feel that anyone who has heard the detailed narratives of the Piegan, giving the names of the killed and injured, as handed down to the present generation and in turn compares them with the account of Lewis, will at once agree that the Gros Ventre had no part in the fight.

It seems probable that the party of Lewis were the first white men to ascend the Marias, yet the tendency of some writers to attribute the subsequent hostility of the Blackfoot and Gros Ventre to the affair with Lewis seems hasty, because they had previously met white men in Canada and elsewhere, but chiefly because the Teton River and the lower Marias were on the Blackfoot frontier where war parties expected to meet enemies. Here the Blackfoot and Gros Ventre fought the Crow and sometimes the Indians west of the mountains. Under such conditions any one found in this region was the logical enemy of the Piegan and Gros Ventre. The fact that this was the place of war seems to indicate that the real territory of the Blackfoot found its extreme southern limit at the head waters of the Cut Bank or Two Medicine River. In this connection, it is of interest to find an editor's note[4] in Larpenteur's journal quoting from the Contributions of the Montana Historical Society, that in the winter of 1830–31 a party of traders went up the Marias, meeting with no Indians until they encountered a war party at the mouth of Badger Creek by whom they were conducted to the nearest camp which was on the Belly River, a branch of the Saskatchewan. The Piegan have definite consistent traditions that the Snake formerly occupied all the streams flowing toward the Missouri, that they were eventually driven

---

[1] Lewis and Clark, 3, 1099 (Coues ed.).
[2] Along the Trail of Lewis and Clark.
[3] Scott, 545.
[4] Larpenteur, 109.

out and that their people did not make definite movements toward the Missouri until horses became numerous among them. Thus, we may pass the consideration of the southern boundary with the statement that all the evidence at hand implies its approximate position before 1800 to have been near the Two Medicine River and eastward, or just below the United States boundary.

The geographical position of the Blackfoot may become clearer from a brief discussion of the tribes holding their frontiers. On the east were the Assiniboine whose territory is defined by Henry as follows:— "They are now numerous, and inhabit a vast extent of plains. Their lands may be said to commence at the Hair hills near Red river, thence running W. along the Assiniboine, from that to the junction of the North and South branches of the Saskatchewan, and up the former branch to Fort Vermillion; then due S. to Battle river, then S. E. to the Missourie, down that river nearly to the Mandane villages, and finally N. E. to the Hair hills again. All this space of open country may be called the lands of the Assiniboines." [1] Hayden[2] has summarized the literature on the Assiniboine and his statements agree fairly well with those of Henry. He places the southwestern limit of their range at Woody Mountains and northwest from that point. This agrees with the line of Henry, as extending southeast from a point on Battle River. The northern boundary is placed at the corresponding branch of the Saskatchewan. (It will be noted that these lines and those defining the territory of the Blackfoot group leave a peculiar triangular area with its base at the Missouri, the ownership of which is not accounted for, probably a place for hunting and war.) Dr. Lowie,[3] in his study of the Assiniboine has made it probable that they occupied this area long before their discovery by the whites and while this does not throw any light on the period of occupation by the Blackfoot group, it is at least suggestive.

The Cree stretched westward like a narrow band through the woods on the north side of the north branch of the Saskatchewan to the northwest as far as the Peace River and the foot hills of the Rocky Mountains. Mackenzie[4] expresses the opinion that the Cree, since the advent of the English on Hudson Bay, pushed out westward in pursuit of beavers and the spoils of war, and by means of their superior arms forced the Athapascan north and the other tribes south. Hayden says that by tradition, the Cree claim to have held this territory as far as Slave and Athabasca Lakes in 1700 and that in 1800 there was a movement of the Assiniboine toward the Missouri.[5]

---

[1] Henry and Thompson, 516.
[2] Hayden, 379.
[3] Vol. 4, Pt. 1, this series.
[4] Mackenzie, lxxvi.
[5] Hayden, 235–248.

These dates are probably quite inexact but in substance agree with the statements of Henry [1] and Harmon. Whatever the facts may be as to previous migrations, it is certain that the western outposts of the Cree were the northern neighbors of the Blackfoot group during the period of 1787 to 1870. Battle River [2] in Henry's time was an interesting point because the Cree were at its mouth, the Assiniboine on its lower course and the Blackfoot on its upper, a condition which doubtless served to perpetuate the name of this stream, for he states that it was traditionally and actually the fighting place of the Cree and the Blackfoot.

On the west was the Great Divide which was certainly a barrier, but the Blackfoot were by no means strangers to those who dwelt beyond. West of Glacier Lake, the Kootenai were to be found. Henry gives some interesting information as to their relations to the Blackfoot.[3] From his post at Rocky Mountain House he ascended the Saskatchewan, crossing the Divide and visiting the Kootenai. Later, he speaks of finding their abandoned lodges on the eastern side out on the edge of the Plains toward Rocky Mountain House. His description of the ruins leaves little room for doubting that the Kootenai had been at that place. Later,[4] he says that similar lodges are found on the Clearwater and other streams. In a matter of fact way, he states that formerly the Kootenai frequented that part of the Plains to make dried provisions. This is quite probable for the buffalo were found by him in and across the range [5] and he speaks of a Kootenai buffalo drive on a cliff, similar to those of the Blackfoot. This writer claims that the Kootenai were driven into the mountains by the tribes from the east. However this may be, the Piegan have traditions of driving the Kootenai westward across the mountains and finally becoming friends. Henry [6] says that the Piegan were the nearest neighbors and friends of the Kootenai. Catlin [7] counts these Kootenai (Cotouné) as a part of the Blackfoot group.

The whole Blackfoot group was perpetually at war with the tribes south of the Kootenai. Here were the Flatheads, Pend d'Oreille, Nez Perce, etc. These tribes seem to have been at peace with each other in the time of Henry, Cox, et. al., and made common cause against the Piegan and Gros Ventre. They did not reside east of the mountains, but resorted there at times to kill the buffalo. All of these tribes and the Snake made annual hunting trips to the head waters of the Missouri. That in the time of Umfreville,

[1] Hayden is not likely to have known the journal of Henry.
[2] Henry and Thompson, 500.
[3] Henry and Thompson, 687.
[4] Henry and Thompson, 703.
[5] Henry and Thompson, 691.
[6] Henry and Thompson, 704.
[7] Catlin, 1, 52.

the great war road of the Blackfoot was toward the Missouri and over into what is now Idaho is implied in his statement as to how they got their horses.[1] Henry's journal makes mention in various places of parties being out in this direction for blood and plunder. This writer takes the view that the brunt of this work fell to the Piegan, and that in consequence of their position they were often attacked by retaliating parties sent by the enemy. The Gros Ventre seem to have been most at war with the Crow and the Assiniboine. Thus, to state the situation figuratively, the Blackfoot group stood with backs to the corner of the Plains formed by the mountains on the west and the forests on the north, facing the hostile Cree, Assiniboine and Crow and also Shoshone, Nez Perce, etc. who threatened to break through the range at the headwaters of the Missouri. At no time in the historic period, however, were they reduced to the mere passive defense of this position, but were ever aggressive from all parts of their frontier.

The geography of the Blackfoot country is interesting. Their range lay between two great water ways leading to mountain portages in the Great Divide. On the north, the Peace River formed a link between the region now known as British Columbia and the Mackenzie Basin. On the south, the Columbia River was reached via the Snake River. Thus, until 1860, at the least, the tides of commerce and immigration rolled harmlessly past their frontiers; but, at last, the cattle men and transcontinental railroads claimed their lands. It may be due to this situation that the Blackfoot have preserved so much of their past culture for, from such accounts as we have, they lived almost untouched until the extinction of the buffalo in 1879 or 1880.[2] It is also significant of their power and numbers that they were able to hold this territory against other powerful tribes that were being crowded out of their traditional hunting grounds in the east.

When the first white men visited the Blackfoot country is not easy to determine. It seems that in 1751 a temporary French post was opened near the present site of Calgary.[3] The change produced by the treaty ending the so-called French and Indian war induced the Hudson Bay and other companies to push into the upper Saskatchewan country as a route to the north and west. About 1790 many houses were established on the north branch. Henry speaks of a pine tree near Rocky Mountain House on which Peter Pangman cut his name in 1790 as marking the western limits of exploration at that time. Rocky Mountain House was established in 1802. It appears from this, that while the Blackfoot may have met with the French they were not in real contact with white traders until about 1790.

---

[1] Umfreville, 197.

[2] Hale, 699.

Bryce, 90.

Buffalo hunting Indians did not appeal to the trader of the old regime: to him no Indian was worthy of consideration unless he produced beaver skins. Henry's journal teems with depreciation of the indolent Slave (Blackfoot, Sarcee and Gros Ventre) who would not kill beaver. The great beaver country, however, was to the north of the north branch and all trading posts on this river were thus in touch with two types of hunters.

With this general sketch of the ethnography of the Blackfoot, we may turn to their origin. One of the first to advance an opinion as to the movements of the Blackfoot, was Mackenzie.[1] He believed them still moving toward the northwest. How he came to this opinion is not stated. Later, Hale regards them as having reached their country by crossing the Plains from the vicinity of the Red River. He states that the Rev. John Maclean, a missionary, made a study of this question and quotes him as follows:— "The former home of these people was in the Red River country, where, from the nature of the soil which blackened their moccasins, they were called Blackfeet." [2] Assuming that this is the Maclean who wrote Canadian Savage Folk, the following may be noted:—"The Blackfeet tell us in their traditional lore that they came in the distant past from the north, from some great lake, supposed to be Lake Winnipeg. When the Bloods, Piegans, and Blackfeet were all one people, living together, and not separated into tribes, as at the present time, the South Piegans,....preferred to live close to the mountains, which they called their home, while the other members of the confederacy dwelt in the north." [3] Hale [4] suggests that the Cree who pushed from the east to Red River forced out the Blackfoot, but quotes M. Lacombe to the effect that the Blackfoot themselves claim to have migrated from the southwest across the Rocky Mountains. Hayden [5] does not discuss the migrations, simply stating that in 1789 they were known to occupy their present country and to have consisted of the same divisions as now. He makes the interesting statement that he has collected a mass of information for a future publication on these people, data which seem to have been lost.

However, the most extended discussion of this question is by Grinnell [6] who takes the opposite view. According to this writer they recently migrated from the north and were once a mountain people. As this is a matter of some importance it seems worth while to examine the evidence offered. Mr. Grinnell is a careful student of the traditional history of the Indian and

---

[1] Mackenzie, lxxi.
[2] Hale, 700.
[3] Maclean, (i), 49.
[4] Hale, 700.
[5] Hayden, 253.
[6] Grinnell, (d), 153.

takes his assumption in the present case from that source. He also notes a tradition, recorded by J. W. Schultz, to the effect that the Blackfoot came from the southwest which may be the same as that known to Lacombe. He, himself, secured traditions and testimony that the people formerly lived north of the Red River and regarded all the country to the south as strange land. Then he proposes that within 200 years they lived in the forests around Lesser Slave Lake "northeast" (?) of their present abode. His evidence is that the Blackfoot name for north is, behind, and for south, before; that the Cree call the Blackfoot, Slaves, and Lesser Slave Lake, the Blackfoot Lake; and on the statements of a few individuals. The latter are in substance, that the people ascended a river, leaving behind a country of timber, finally coming in sight of mountains and going into them to live. Let us consider in turn the interpretations given these facts.

When first observed the Blackfoot appear as a large nation in process of expansion and doubtless forcing out their borders. Naturally, the Piegan by virtue of their position would have traditions of a southward migration and the introduction of the horse must have turned the eyes of all toward the south and southeast. Then, as the associations between names and directions are not absolute, the peculiar relation expressed in the Blackfoot language may be accidental. That the Piegan, from whom most of Grinnell's information seems to have come, now refer everything to the north, is natural because their larger reservation is south of their former home. As to the term Slave, the writer has not found opportunity for investigation. Henry speaks of the Blackfoot and Gros Ventre as Slaves, but he seems to be the only writer of journals during the fur trade period who makes such use of the term. The editor [1] comments on this peculiar use of the term but can give no information respecting it. The term, however, seems to have been current among later traders and to have been applied with considerable freedom. Mackenzie states:— "When this country was formerly invaded by the Knisteneaux [Cree], they found the Beaver Indians inhabiting the land about Portage la Loche; [near Methy Lake], and the adjoining tribe were those whom they called slaves. They drove both these tribes before them: when the latter proceeded down the river from the lake of the hills [Lake Athabasca], in consequence of which that part of it obtained the name of Slave River. The former proceeded up the river; and when the Knisteneaux made peace with them, this place [Peace Point near mouth of Peace River] was settled to be the boundary." [2] Since Mackenzie speaks of the divisions of the Blackfoot under their proper names

---

[1] Henry and Thompson, 523.
[2] Mackenzie, 123.

and when he explains the term Slave [1] makes no mention of its application to tribes to the south otherwise known to him, it appears strange that Henry should use the term. Yet Mackenzie's explanation that the term was employed by the Cree as one of reproach makes it probable that it may then have been suggested to traders as a class name for the Blackfoot and their neighbors. There are not wanting other instances of such naming, and taking everything into consideration, this seems the most probable. The analogy between the Cree name of "Little Slaves" and Lesser Slave Lake, has appealed to Grinnell as a strong point in the support of his views that the whole of the Blackfoot formerly lived at that place. So far we fail to see just grounds for taking the distribution of the term Slave in geographical nomenclature as evidence for the former correlated distribution of the Blackfoot. On the other hand, if the Mackenzie statement is to be taken, the conclusion of Grinnell that the Blackfoot lived next south of the Beaver Indians would imply that they resided in the vicinity of the Blackfoot Hills, or at the mouth of the Vermillion River. This brings us back to our former definition of boundaries and to the edge of the Plains. Thus, while we find no actual disproof of Mr. Grinnell's theory, it does not seem quite consistent with other data.

We collected traditions bearing upon the above points which seem to be inconsistent with the theory that the Blackfoot formerly lived in the northern forests. The Piegan, especially, claim that they came up from the south from a region beyond, or to the west, of the mountains and that they formerly lived north of their present reservation, sometimes wintering in the foothills, among the trees. The incidents in some of their myths, especially those of the Old Man, are often definitely located in the north, but this north is in all cases placed between Macleod and Edmonton, within the territory assigned to the Blackfoot in the previous discussion. The Piegan claim that before the white man dominated their country (an uncertain date, probably 1750–1840) the Blackfoot, Blood, and Piegan lived north of Macleod; the Kootenai in the vicinity of the present Blood Reserve; the Gros Ventre and the Assiniboine to the east of the Kootenai; the Snake on the Teton River, and as far north as Two Medicine River; and the Flatheads on the Sun River. These traditions were so definite and consistent that consideration must be given them. The other point of interest is that the traditional expansion of the Blackfoot that drove all these beyond the Mountains or elsewhere came after the introduction of the horse.[2] Before taking up the discussion of this point, it is well to note that we made inquiry as to traditions of trading upon Hudson's Bay and other posts in that direction. No such traditions

---

[1] Mackenzie, 3.

[2] Maclean, (i), 597, claims that the Snake were driven out of Alberta by the Blackfoot.

exist for posts beyond the Forks, and nothing of a definite nature for points east of Old Fort Vermillion. The Northern Blackfoot claim to have received their first knowledge of white men from the Cree and themselves to have met them near Edmonton.

We may conclude that the migration of the Blackfoot from the north as claimed by Grinnell, is proven only for the territory previously defined and that there is very little data for the assumption that they moved down from the forests still further north. The fact that they lived in the extreme northern part of the Plains and were more or less familiar with the forest must be taken into account when assigning probable weight to the foregoing traditions of such residence.[1] At any rate, the definite tradition that the Blackfoot came from across the mountains is equally valid when taken alone with the tradition favored by Grinnell. We have seen that there is little direct data to support either. This is a matter of considerable importance, for acceptance of the view that the Blackfoot lived farther north would make them a forest people; whereas so far, practically no traces of such a life are to be found in their traditional culture. The habitat we have defined is well within the Plains, and their southern movement seems to have been the modern tendency toward the Missouri, beginning with the establishment of trading posts in that area. In general, no satisfactory evidence has come to hand that the Blackfoot ever occupied other definite territory than their historic habitat, defined in the preceding pages. A more exhaustive discussion of this problem will be undertaken at another time.

The tradition that the pushing out into the Upper Missouri region was after the introduction of the horse suggests inquiring as to the time of this occurrence. Grinnell [2] states that tribal tradition places the date for the introduction of the horse "in the very earliest years of the present century" (1800), but this is contradictory to historical evidence. Umfreville was near the mouth of the Red Deer River in 1784–7 and states most emphatically that the Blackfoot were well supplied with horses. The elder Henry [3] in 1776 saw among the Assiniboine "one of those herds of horses which the Osinipoilles possess in numbers." The same writer states that, "Such of the Cristinaux as inhabit the plains, have also their horses, like the Osinipoilles." He did not meet the Blackfoot but heard the Assiniboine speak of them as a powerful nation with whom they were at war. Now, it seems quite probable that if the Cree and Assiniboine were well supplied with horses in 1776 their war-like neighbors on the west were likewise the owners

---

[1] Henry's statement that one band lived entirely in the wooded foot-hills of the mountains on the west should be considered when reading Grinnell's statement of traditions.

[2] Grinnell, (a), 177.

[3] Henry, 289, 299.

of horses. Thus we have evidence of horses among the Blackfoot in 1784 and good reason for assuming that they were introduced at an earlier date. The journal of Henry and Thompson makes constant mention of horses. Of the tribes west of the Mountains, the Nez Perce [1] are mentioned as well provided with them and the presence of wild horses, "frequently seen in the large gangs," in the Kootenai country is noted.[2]   Teit [3] asserts that horses were known in the Thompson River country "towards the end of the eighteenth century."   Clark [4] quotes a letter from Father Ravalli to the effect that the Pend D'Oreille saw horses "about one hundred and forty years since."   The time of writing is not given but was before 1885, which would place the date at about 1745.   Such seems to be the nature of the data upon which any determination of the time for the introduction of the horse among the Blackfoot must be based.   While quite unsatisfactory, it indicates the probable date as earlier than 1776.   Once, when discussing the subject, an Indian made a suggestive remark to the writer.   He said, in substance, that it often happened that a whole tribe or part of a tribe was, due to some accident, hostile raid or gambling mania, deprived of horses for a season or two and that some of the traditions and observations recorded in books doubtless referred to such events rather than to the first introduction of the horse.   Our traditional information is, in effect, that the Piegan received horses first from the Snake and Flathead Indians, that this was long before white men came to their country and that the time was about two hundred years ago.

---

[1] Henry and Thompson, 712.
[2] Henry and Thompson, 708.
[3] Teit, 257.
[4] Clark, 300.

Food Habits.

No one seems to have made an exhaustive study of the food of the Blackfoot when they were living their free life. They have no traditions of agriculture and seem to have been a hunting people for many generations, depending chiefly upon the buffalo and other large mammals. Like other non-agricultural plains tribes, however, they consumed a considerable amount of vegetable food. One of the earliest observers says, "their chief subsistence is the flesh of buffaloes, the deer species and likewise vegetables."[1] A very satisfactory statement of Blackfoot vegetable foods has been made by Grinnell,[2] in which are enumerated the following: service berries, *Amelanchier alnifolia*; wild cherries, *Prunus demissa*; bull berries, *Shepherdia argentea*; red willow berries; camas root, *Camassia esculenta*; prairie turnip, *Psoralea esculenta*; bitter root; and buds of the wild rose, *Rosa cinnamomea*.[3] According to statements of the Blackfoot, the prairie turnip was seldom found north of the Sun River and the camas root rarely east of the foothills of the mountains in Montana. Thus, these important foods were accessible only in the extreme southern part of their historic habitat. On the other hand, in their opinion, the service berry was the most important vegetable food, reference to its gathering and curing being frequent in ceremonies and narratives. In general, while the quantity of vegetable food consumed was considerable, it is well to note that such food was in a large part compounded with the flesh of buffalo or animals of the deer kind, flesh being the primary food.

Umfreville notes a taboo on certain kinds of animal foods: "they will eat no kind of water-fowl, amphibious animal, or fish." [4] From our own information, we infer that this statement is too sweeping, since such food was taken when the flesh of mammals was not at hand. The flesh of the bear was usually regarded as too sacred to be eaten.[5] Dogs were not eaten,

---

[1] Umfreville, 202.

[2] Grinnell, (a) 203.

[3] After this was written a very complete list was published by McClintock (277) with some different identifications:— service berry, *Amelanchier oblongifolia;* buffalo berry, *Elaeagnus argentea;* berries of *Disporum trachycarpum;* cow parsnip, *Heracleum lanatum;* wild potato, *Claytonia lanceolata;* smart weed, *Polygonum bistortoides;* wild onion, *Albium recurvatum;* Carolina milk vetch, *Astragalus carolinianus;* bitter root, *Lewisa rediviva;* wild mint, *Mentha canadensis;* wild turnip, *Lithospermum linearifolium;* evening primrose, *Musenium divaricatum*. With the exception of the first two and mint, the roots were the parts eaten.

[4] Umfreville, 202.

[5] See also Maximilian, 252: "They feed on almost every kind of animal except the grizzly bear * * * * and they have an aversion to amphibious animals."

though the modern intrusive society of the Hair-parters, makes some pretense of serving them at ceremonies.   At present, fish and fowls are eaten when at hand.

According to Henry, "They [Piegan] have no particular hour for meals: all day meat of some kind is on the fire." [1]   When economic conditions permit, this is the present practice.

Methods of Preparation.   The methods of preparing food are usually of considerable ethnographical interest.   During the berry season, the Blackfoot camps were shifted to favorable localities where the women and girls worked industriously gathering the fruit into rectangular rawhide bags, or similar bags of soft dressed skin, which when filled, were emptied into

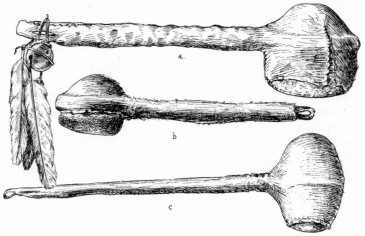

Fig. 1 *b* (50–5854), *c* (50–6433).   Types of Mauls.   Length of *a*, 46 cm.

larger storage bags.   The gathered fruit was taken to camp and dried in the sun, after which it was stored in parfleche or other bags.   According to Grinnell,[2] service berries were beaten from the bushes, falling upon a robe or blanket, a reference to which occurs in our myth of the Old Man (page 29, Vol. 2).

The wild cherry was gathered when ripe and pounded on a stone until the fruit with its pits was reduced to a thick paste.   This was dried and packed away in bags or used in making pemmican.   While this dried mess was sometimes eaten alone, it was more often used in soups.   For pounding

[1] Henry and Thompson, 724.
[2] Grinnell, (a), 203.

the cherries a hammer was used. These hammers were of stone, usually hafted to wooden handles by shrunken rawhide. One specimen in the Museum collection, Fig. 1c, was obtained from the woman who made it. The head is of stone, egg-shaped, and has a transverse groove around the middle. The handle is of wood, apparently double, passing around the head in the groove. Over the whole, is a firm covering of rawhide. The entire head, except the mere surface of contact, is covered. At the end of the handle is a small loop for a cord. The woman stated that she found the stone already grooved. She had never heard of anyone shaping or grooving them, always using such as were found around old camp sites. The collection contains another specimen, showing marks of long usage. Another very old specimen is somewhat heavier and has a head of different shape (Fig. 1a). There is also a small pounder with a short handle (Fig. 1b). The stone head is of irregular shape, somewhat pointed at the top, grooved around the middle and covered with calfskin. This specimen seems to be of recent manufacture. While, as stated above, such hammers were often used in smashing cherries, their chief function seems to have been the breaking of bones in order to obtain the marrow.

Edible roots were formerly gathered with the digging stick, an instrument now surviving only in ceremonies. Prairie turnips were often peeled, strung and hung up to dry, though a great many were consumed in the raw state. Again, the dried turnip was pounded fine and used for thickening soup. Camas was usually roasted at the gathering camp, dried in the sun and stored. In general, it may be said that practically all kinds of vegetable foods were dried and stored.[1]

It is a singular fact that most peoples possess some important article of diet corresponding to the bread of European races: for example, in America, the Californians used acorn meal, the agricultural Indians, corn meal, etc. While the Blackfoot had no cereal from which such bread substance could be made, they found a substitute in a compound of berries and flesh generally known as pemmican. For this, the best cuts of buffalo were dried in the usual manner. Then they were pounded on a stone until fine. Hammers, as previously described, were often used for this purpose. Just before pounding, the pieces of dried meat were held over the fire to make them soft and oily. Marrow and other fats were heated and mixed with the pounded meats, after which crushed wild cherries were worked into the mess. Often, a few leaves from the peppermint plant were added in order to give flavor to it. The whole was then packed into parfleche or

---

[1] Further details are given by Grinnell, (a), 203. Unless otherwise indicated, all references to other writers are cited as confirming information secured by us except where comparative data are introduced

other bags, a compact sticky mass, easily preserved and good for eating without further preparation. While the flesh of the buffalo was preferred for pemmican that of deer and elk would be used if at hand. The marrow fat was obtained by boiling cracked bones and skimming the floating fat from the top of the kettle with a dipper made of horn.[1] As among many tribes, such marrow fat or grease, was often stored in bladders.[2] The following specific statement of the above process may be added:—

"Pemmican is manufactured in the following manner: The choicest cuts of meat are selected and cut into flakes and dried. Then all the marrow is collected and the best of the tallow, which are dissolved together over a slow fire to prevent burning. Many tribes use berries in their pemmican. Mountaineers always do unless they have sugar. The meat is now pulverized to the consistency of mince

Fig. 2.   Meat drying Rack.

meat; the squaws generally doing this on a flat rock, using a pestle, many specimens of which may be seen on exhibition in museums. A layer of meat is spread, about two inches thick, the squaws using a wooden dipper, a buffalo horn, or a claw for this work. On this meat is spread a certain amount of ingredients made from the marrow and tallow, the proportion depending on the taste. This same process is repeated until the required amount is secured. One pound of pemmican is equal to five pounds of meat.

---

[1] For another account see Grinnell, (a), 207.   Franklin, 104, observed the Cree beating dried meat spread on a rawhide, with a stone.
[2] For such a decorated bag of the Gros Ventre, see Kroeber, (a), 167.

Buffalo tongues are split the long way and dried for future use, and thus prepared are a delicacy fit for a prince." [1]

In early days, the great fur companies of the northwest consumed a great deal of dried meat. To meet this demand, the Indians supplied a kind of pemmican, packed in large bags sealed with tallow. In buffalo days, the Blackfoot produced a great deal of this material. For their own use, they often stored buffalo meat, cut into small pieces and mixed with dried and toasted back-fat.

Meats not made into pemmican nor consumed while fresh, were dried for storage or other purposes. The flesh was cut into large thin slices and hung up to cure in the wind and sun. In order that it might be out of the reach of dogs a scaffold of poles was erected, similar to that shown in Fig. 2. In recent years a simple rack was much used. (Plate II.) At night, the meat was either covered or taken into the tipi to protect it from moisture. The flesh of cattle is dried in the same manner. Such dried meat was sometimes eaten without further treatment, though it was usually toasted over the fire or even fried in a pan.

Back-fat and suet did not keep well unless partly cooked before drying. A special form of back-fat, used by the Blackfoot and other tribes, has been given the name "depuyer" (depouille), a good description of which has been given by Hamilton:—

"Another important article of food, the equal of which is not to be had except from the buffalo, is "depuyer" (depouille). It is a fat substance that lies along the backbone; next to the hide, running from the shoulder-blade to the last rib, and is about as thick as one's hand or finger. It is from seven to eleven inches broad; tapering to a feather edge on the lower side. It will weigh from five to eleven pounds, according to the size and condition of the animal. This substance is taken off and dipped in hot grease for half a minute, then is hung up inside of a lodge to dry and smoke for twelve hours. It will keep indefinitely, and is used as a substitute for bread, but is superior to any bread that was ever made. It is eaten with the lean and dried meat, and is tender and sweet and very nourishing, for it seems to satisfy the appetite. When going on the war-path the Indians would take some dried meat and some depuyer to live on, and nothing else, not even if they were to be gone for months." [2]

Cooking. The cookery of the Blackfoot may be considered under the heads of roasting and boiling. Under the former, we shall place all methods not making direct use of vessels. Vegetable food was often roasted or baked. The prairie turnip was baked in hot ashes. The camas root re-

---

[1] Hamilton, 32. While this account is not given as peculiar to the Blackfoot, the details closely agree with our information.

[2] Hamilton, 32.

ceived more elaborate treatment in which were manifested certain social and ceremonial functions. According to our information, men were supposed to keep at some distance from the cooking place. First, a hole about ten feet square and three feet deep was dug. Stones, very hot, were placed over the bottom and covered with wet willow leaves and branches. On this, the camas roots were placed, each woman dividing her portion from the others. Willow brush was placed on the top and earth heaped over it. On this earth the fire was built and carefully tended for thirty-six hours or more, until the odor from the baking camas indicated the end. The fire was then raked away and the camas uncovered, at which a cloud of steam arose. The roots were then taken out and what was not eaten on the spot was dried and put in bags for storage. Should any of the individual portions of camas be burned, ill-luck would most certainly befall the woman to whom they belonged — "some of her relatives would die soon." [1]

While meats were preferred boiled, there were other methods in common use. According to Henry [2] meat was often roasted on a spit or broiled on coals. Our information indicates this to be true, especially in the case of ribs. The large intestine, cut in sections and dried, was broiled over coals, and occasionally sections of the smaller intestines, blown up with air and tied at the ends, were prepared by broiling over a fire. Again, a section of the large intestine was filled with blood and fat, the ends tied and the whole roasted by covering with hot ashes. It was turned about and tested from time to time with a pointed stick.

A preparation called Crow-Indian-guts was regarded as a luxury. A section of the small intestine was cleaned and drawn over a long strip of meat, the ends tied and the whole held over the coals supported by a stick. Care was required to keep the intestine from bursting and permitting the juices of the meat to escape.

A method of cooking in a hole was sometimes used for meats. At the time of the buffalo drive, a hole might be dug in the ground, many hot stones placed in the bottom and over these a layer of willow branches and grass. Next, a layer or two of feotal and newly born calves over which again were spread branches, grass and finally earth. This was spoken of as a dry cook. The hole was usually filled in the evening and by the following day it would be ready to uncover. A variation of this was similar to the mode of roasting camas. A hole was dug to the depth of four spans of the thumb and fore finger and lined with hot stones and brush as before. Dressed calves were wrapped in fresh hides, two hides spread over the brush, water

---

[1] Grinnell, (a), 204, gives a similar account.
[2] Henry and Thompson, 724.

poured in, the calves quickly placed and the whole covered with two more fresh hides. The upper hide was stretched and staked. Then earth was heaped over all and a fire kindled on top. .

Eggs of water fowl were sometimes cooked in a hole with hot stones as described by Grinnell.[1] No one seemed to have heard of a method of cooking eggs in a bark tube as described by McDougall.[2]

Boiling seems to have been the favorite Blackfoot method of preparing food and they were especially fond of soups. The preparation of such food necessitated cooking vessels of some sort. It is not certain that the Blackfoot ever made pottery, though some individuals claim such information to have been handed down to the present generation. An old woman had heard that cooking pots were once made of pulverized rock and some sticky material. She never heard of pots hollowed out of stone. A man had heard that pots were made a long time ago. They were fashioned of mud and sand. A bag of rawhide was filled with sand, greased on the outside and the pot shaped over it. The sand was then poured out and the bag withdrawn. The pot was filled with fat and hung over the fire to harden. When finished, it was tested by boiling water in it. Such pots grew gradually harder with use.[3] They were supported by a rawhide cord passing around the rim. The cord had to be changed often. He also heard that pipes were formerly made of clay and hardened by holding over the fire. During this operation they were always kept rubbed with fat. Aside from these narratives, there is no evidence that pottery was made by the Blackfoot. That these statements may represent intrusive traditions is suggested by their seeming parallels among the Gros Ventre [4] and certain striking agreements with processes employed by the Mandan and other village Indians. Ever since the advent of the fur trade, they have used kettles of iron, copper and brass. In the tipis, these kettles were formerly hung from tripods of wood by a wooden hook. In later years, a single rod with a curved top, ending in a hook, was in general use.

Methods of boiling without pottery vessels were known and practised. Men on war parties or other expeditions of hazard prepared their meals in such manner as conditions permitted, but, as one informant expressed it, it was difficult to get on without some kind of soup, especially blood soup. This is the kind of soup referred to in the story of the Blood Clot Boy. Old people, women as well as men, frequently testified that such soup was best when prepared by the methods used on war or hunting parties. This

---

[1] Grinnell, (a), 207.
[2] McDougall, 57.
[3] For a similar statement in a myth, see Vol. 2, 43.
[4] Kroeber, (a), 150.

method was to boil in a fresh hide or paunch by means of hot stones. We observed an old man demonstrating the process of which photographic illustrations are shown in Plate I.

In this case, four sticks about 40 cm. in length were driven into the ground on a radius of about 15 cm. Near the top of each stake was a kind of catch, or notch, the but of a projecting twig or branch. The fresh paunch of a cow was brought out, a slit cut in the edge with a knife and thrust down over one of the stakes. A second slit was cut near this one, the edge of the paunch given a twist and slipped over the stick once more. In a similar manner, the edge of the paunch was adjusted to the other stakes at such points as gave it the form of a bag. The form of this bag was then improved by the addition of two other stakes similar to the four first placed. The bag was still a little too loose but was quickly adjusted by turning an edge over the top of a stake. The rough surface of the paunch was on the outside. A stone about the size of an egg was placed gently in the bottom of the bag which now just touched the ground. The demonstrator said that it would boil quickly if the bottom touched the ground and that the stone served to keep the bag in place. About a quart of blood with an equal amount of water was poured in. In the meantime, a number of stones had been heated in a fire of wood and cow chips. A stick about 60 cm. long with a forked end and a stick similar to those supporting the paunch were used to carry the hot stones. From time to time, these were gently slid into the soup which was stirred with the shorter stick. The cook tested the mess now and then, by licking the end of the stirring stick. When the soup threatened to boil over, a little water was poured into it. It was stated that other kinds of soup were made in such a vessel, as berry soup and common meat soup.

When a paunch was not at hand a fresh hide might be used in the same manner, though the usual procedure was to depress it into a hole in the ground.[1] The edges of the hide were held in place by stakes, but if these were not at hand stones were laid around to hold it by their weight or, if there were several in the party, knives were stuck through the hide after the manner of stakes. The hide was used for boiling meat, the paunch rarely for anything but soup.

According to one informant, should the buffalo be killed in a sheltered spot, the entrails would be removed, the carcass turned on its back with blood and fat in the cavity, a little water added and hot stones dropped in, thus producing a rich soup within the carcass itself. This, however, seems to have been an unusual method.

Utensils. Culinary and other utensils seem to have been made of wood,

---

[1] Grinnell, (a), 205.

horn and skins. The Northern Blackfoot seem to have some knowledge of birch bark but this may be the result of observation when in contact with their northern neighbors.[1] The Piegan, at least, seem to have no knowledge of its use among their ancestors. There is no satisfactory evidence that basketry was one of their arts, though the Piegan claim to have made some crude fish traps. At present, a great many so-called Nez Perce bags are found in use, but these are secured by barter from the Indians west of the mountains.

Though we found no specimens, wooden bowls were formerly in use for serving and eating. Large knots from any tree except the cottonwood were used in their manufacture. First, the outside was trimmed to agree with the general form of a bowl. Then the hollow was made with a hatchet or a piece of iron, shaped like a chisel. When the cavity was about the proper shape and size a red hot stone was dropped in and made to roll or slide round and round until the surface was smooth and even. It was then scraped with a stone chip or metal scraper. The outside was not burned but worked into shape by scraping. The surface was then given a coat of grease and polished by heating and rubbing. In more recent times augurs and chisels were used to work out the cavity. An early account states that:—
"Their culinary utensils are few and very rough. Wooden dishes of different dimensions are made of aspen or poplar knots; spoons are formed of the same material, or more commonly of buffalo's or ram's horn. Some of the latter are very large, holding about two quarts, and answer as both dish and spoon." [2] Wooden bowls are still used in certain ceremonies, especially those connected with the medicine pipe, but are almost without exception bought of white traders. The collection contains a flat, oval wooden dish of peculiar shape which, while probably of Indian make, seems to have been cut from a large commercial machine-made wooden bowl. However, it is provided with a hanger of thong like other Indian bowls and cups. According to Grinnell, "Basins or flat dishes were sometimes made of mountain sheep horn, boiled, split, and flattened, and also of split buffalo horn, fitted and sewed together with sinew, making a flaring, saucer-shaped dish. These were used as plates or eating dishes. Of course, they leaked a little for the joints were not tight." [3]

Spoons were made of wood, bone, or horn. The collection contains a curious spoon made of bone, apparently from the pelvis of a calf (Fig. 3b). The bowl is very shallow, the end is drilled and a small thong is tied through it. Though many spoons of neat and convenient form were made of buffalo

---

[1] For mention of bark dishes in a myth see Vol. 2, 210.
[2] Henry and Thompson, 724.
[3] Grinnell, (a), 203.

horn, the most of these have passed out of use.   The collection contains a slender spoon apparently made of cow horn (Fig. 3c).   The base of the horn has been split so as to give it a long slender graceful bowl, and the handle has been formed by bending the tip.   The shape of the handle is such, that when the spoon is held between the thumb and finger it fits easily into the

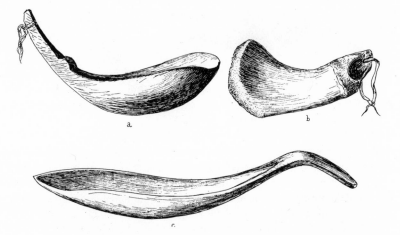

Fig. 3 *a* (50–5853), *b* (50–7), *c* (50–9).   Types of Spoons.   Length of *a*, 19 cm.

hand.   There is also a small buffalo horn spoon, of similar shape, Fig. 3a, seemingly of recent manufacture.   The handle of this specimen has not been bent as in the preceding.   From these specimens, we get the impression that the former (Fig. 3c) was the typical form of the small buffalo horn spoon used by the Blackfoot.

Large ladles or dippers were fashioned of mountain sheep horn.   Such specimens are now exceedingly rare.   The few now used rarely have handles, and have the appearance of dippers broken from their handles.   About the only occasion of their present use, is in the ceremonies connected with the medicine women at the sun dance.   The collection also contains a dipper made of the large end of a mountain sheep horn (Fig. 4).   It may have had a handle at one time, but this is not certain.   A hole is drilled at one end through which a section of thong is tied.   Our failure to collect specimens with long handles as found among other tribes, suggests the scarcity of the long-handled horn type among the Blackfoot.[1]

The process of shaping horn spoons was simple.   First, the horn was

---

[1] Maximilian figures one of this type for the Upper Missouri, 250.

scorched in the fire, causing the gluey matter to fry out, and then trimmed down to the correct shape with a knife. The horn was then boiled in water until soft. Then a stone of suitable shape was forced into the part for the bowl, the latter being held in place by the sides of a hole in the ground. The handle was bent as desired and weighted down with stones. When thor-

Fig. 4 (50–4572). A Dipper. Length, 31 cm.

oughly dry these were removed, the spoon then being ready for use. Both men and women made spoons and bowls.

Buffalo horns were sometimes carried as drinking cups. One specimen secured is provided with a cord for slinging over the shoulder. The tip is ornamented with beadwork and the body of the horn with rows of brass headed nails. Water was formerly carried in bags of paunch or bladder. Mention of these was made by Henry [1] but by far the best statement is by Grinnell:—

"The Blackfeet made buckets, cups, basins, and dishes from the lining of the buffalo's paunch. This was torn off in large pieces, and was stretched over a flattened willow or cherry hoop at the bottom and top. These hoops were sometimes inside and sometimes outside the bucket or dish. In the latter case, the hoop at the bottom was often sewed to the paunch, which came down over it, double on the outside, the needle holes being pitched with gum or tallow. The hoop at the upper edge was also sewed to the paunch, and a rawhide bail passed under it, to carry it by.

These buckets were shaped somewhat like our wooden ones, and were of different sizes, some of them holding four or five gallons. They were more or less flexible, and when carried in a pack, they could be flattened down like a crush hat, and so took up but little room. If set on the ground when full, they would stand up for a while, but as they soon softened and fell down, they were usually hung up by the bail on a little tripod. Cups were made in the same way as buckets, but on a smaller scale and without the bail. Of course, nothing hot could be placed in these vessels." [2]

Spoons and bowls were usually carried in bags of buffalo skin, dressed with the hair on.

[1] Henry and Thompson. 724.
[2] Grinnell, (a), 201–2.

As to what kinds of knives were used before fur-trading days, can be little more than conjectured, yet some interesting information was obtained. The people claim that bone and stone were used. In speaking of certain myths and ceremonies reference is often made to a "white-rock knife." [1] A large leaf-shaped flaked blade was given us under this name (Fig. 5b). It had been picked up from the surface of the ground and the claim was made that such blades were occasionally found. While this specimen is probably not a knife, it may be taken as a suggestion as to the kind of knife referred to in tradition. In the discussion of skin dressing it will be shown that the use of stone implements is not quite extinct (p. 66). Even in recent times, parties out for horse stealing occasionally found themselves far from home without knives. Sometimes the metal band from the but of a gun would be removed and sharpened on a stone. One man stated that he once found himself without a knife. He shot a buffalo calf which he dressed with flakes

Fig. 5 a (20.0–1500), b (50–4536). Stone Knives. Length of a, 8 cm.

struck from a bluish pebble. At another time, he showed us some chips from an ancient camp site similar to those he used (Fig. 5a). According to his testimony such a resort to stone knives was not infrequent.

Bone was used for points and probably for knives. The Museum collection contains what was said to be the model of a bone knife. It is a section of a cow's rib, the grip wrapped with undressed calf skin and one edge made keen by scraping. One peculiarity of the shape is the square end, causing the cutting edge to terminate in a point that seems sharp enough to cut flesh readily (Fig. 6).

At present, every woman is provided with a commercial ax, one of the most important household utensils. It is used in providing wood, cutting through the joints of large pieces of meat, cracking bones, driving stakes, etc. From the information at hand, it appears that this instrument has displaced the stone hammer shown in Fig. 1a. With such a hammer, dry branches could be broken readily, bones cracked, tipis staked down, etc.

---

[1] Vol. 2, 41, 56, 75, etc.

No definite information could be secured as to aboriginal modes of making fire, but according to Grinnell, this was by forms of wood friction.[1] Flint and steel is still in occasional use. Suitable stone was found in parts of their country and steel was secured by trade. The older type of steel is shown in Fig. 7, which, according to its owner, had been in the family for generations. For tinder, various forms of dry fungi were used. According to Grinnell, a fungus found on birch trees was preferred;[2] but according to

Fig. 6 (50–6). A bone Knife. Length, 30 cm.

our information, the preference was given to a large bulbous variety growing on the ground often called, "the fallen stars," or "dusty stars."[3] With the introduction of the flint and steel, methods of preserving fire seem to have fallen into disuse. Grinnell states that in ancient times, fire was carried in a buffalo horn and fed from time to time with punk.[4]

Fires were usually kindled with fragments of small dead branches. For many purposes, the bark of the cotton-wood was preferred, because it burned

Fig. 7 (50–6457). A Steel for striking Fire.

with very little smoke. Henry says of the Piegan:— "Many families are still destitute of either a kettle or an ax. The women, who are mere slaves, have much difficulty in collecting firewood. Those who have no axes fasten together the ends of two long poles, which two women then hook over dry limbs of large trees, and thus break them off. They also use lines for the same purpose; a woman throws a line seven or eight fathoms long over a dry limb, and jerks it until the limb breaks off. Others again set fire to

---

[1] Grinnell, (a), 200.
[2] Grinnell, (a), 201.
[3] See myth, Vol. 2, 42.
[4] Grinnell, (a), 201.

the roots of large trees, which having burned down, the branches supply a good stock of fuel. The trunk is seldom attacked by those who have axes, as chopping blisters their hands." [1]   Brushwood for summer use is still gathered by the women, though they are by no means averse to chopping heavy branches with an ax. Among the Blood and Northern Blackfoot, slender dead branches are set up on end in a conical stack about the size of a tipi, a form of wood pile common in central Canada.

Hunting. Naturally, the killing of buffalo was of the greatest economic importance to the Blackfoot. The habits of this animal doubtless invited co-operative hunting, especially before the introduction of the horse. While in later days, the Blackfoot occasionally made use of the horse-surround, it remains that the so-called drive was the most elaborate method of buffalo hunting. Tradition and ceremony bear testimony to the antiquity of this custom, but the introduction of firearms and the subsequent gradual diminution of the buffalo led to its abandonment. Umfreville, who evidently came in touch with the Blackfoot, gives a good account of a drive, but apparently not as observed among the Blackfoot. The earliest authentic descriptive note is by Henry:—

"Another party of young men endeavored to impound the buffalo, but the weather continued unfavorable; the fog did not clear away until toward evening, and the wind was still contrary. A principal chief of a neighboring pound came to invite us to his camp, where he said the buffalo were numerous; but old Painted Feather would not consent to our going. The day passed, no buffalo came, and we had only the satisfaction of viewing the mangled carcasses strewn about in the pound. The bulls were mostly entire, none but good cows having been cut up. The stench from this inclosure was·great, even at this season, for the weather was mild. *22d.* We were called early to see the buffalo, and instantly were on the look-out hill, whence we saw plenty indeed; but the wind was still unfavorable, and every herd that was brought near the ranks struck off in a wrong direction. We could plainly discern the young men driving whole herds from different directions, until these came within scent of the smoke, when they dispersed. We remained until noon, when I lost all patience, and came away much disappointed. The Indians desired us to remain, as they were certain of getting at least one herd in before dark; but I would not listen to them. After a pleasant ride, we reached home at four o'clock, having run several races on the road. *23d.* Some Blackfeet arrived from the camp where I had been, bringing a quantity of fat meat. They informed me we had scarcely left when a large herd was brought in; they had called to us, but we did not hear, as we were too busy racing." [2]

This is certainly unsatisfactory, but should be used in connection with the same writer's fine account of Assiniboine drives,[3] worded in a manner

---

[1] Henry and Thompson, 724.
[2] Henry and Thompson, 577.
[3] Henry and Thompson, 518.

that indicates his having witnessed them on more than one occasion. From Henry's style and method, it seems safe to infer that had the Blackfoot pound possessed material differences he would have noted the fact. The place visited by him was on the Vermillion River, the camp of a division of the Northern Blackfoot. This assumption that this was a pound of the Assiniboine type is supported by Henry's remarks concerning the Piegan:—

"So much do these people abhor work that, to avoid the trouble of making proper pounds, they seek some precipice along the bank of the river, to which they extend their ranks and drive the buffalo headlong over it. If not killed or entirely disabled from the fall, the animals are generally so much bruised as to be easily dispatched with the bow and arrow. But this method sometimes proves dangerous; for if the leading buffalo, coming to the edge of the precipice, is not entirely exhausted, she may refuse to make the leap, suddenly turn about, and break through the ranks, followed by the whole herd, carrying before them everything which offers to obstruct their progress. No effort of man suffices to arrest a herd in full carreer after the cow that leads them; and thus lives are sometimes lost, as the natives standing near the precipice, to form the ranks and see the buffalo tumble down, have no time to get out of the way." [1]

The accounts of later writers are all based upon informants. Thus, it appears that while Henry did not see the pounds of the Piegan type and had very little experience with either of them, he is the only available observer. The most complete later account is by Grinnell, from data collected among Indians and frontiersmen. He supports our inference from Henry, by attributing to the Northern Blackfoot pounds like those of the Cree and different from those of the Blood and Piegan.[2] The method of the Plains Cree was about the same as that employed by the Assiniboine.

We secured from Indians, information as to the essential features of Blood and Piegan drives. On the Blackfoot reserve in Montana, are several places regarded by the Indians as sites of buffalo drives. Similar sites are to be found on the Blood reserve in Alberta. The writer made a careful examination of a site on Two Medicine River, almost due south from Browning. On the south side of the stream is a flat bordered by a bluff about twenty meters high. The highest part of the bluff stands between two systems of coulees, or drains, whose heads enclose a large tract of grass land. We made a rough sketch of the site, showing the relation of the stream and flat to the bluff (Fig. 8). From the highest part of the bluff peculiar piles of boulders extend outward toward the grass land. While these boulders are somewhat scattered, their former positions are indicated by a nucleus of ten or more, often deeply imbedded in the surface

[1] Henry and Thompson, 725.
[2] Grinnell, (a), 230.

soil. These piles are arranged in somewhat irregular lines as seen in the
diagram. The distances between the respective piles vary from three to
seven meters, increasing as the line extends outward from the bluff. The
line to the left can be traced about two miles and the one to the right,
about half that distance, though both become very indistinct and uncertain

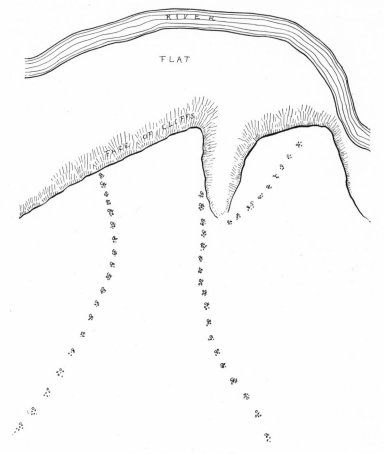

Fig. 8.   Plan of a Buffalo Pound.

as their limits are approached.   As shown in the diagram, there is a secondary line on the right skirting a break in the bluff caused by one of the flank-
ing coulees mentioned at the beginning of this description.   Thus, it will be
seen that the two main lines of rock piles enclose an irregular V whose apex

is below the edge of the bluff. The distance between them near the top of the bluff is about fifty meters.

It is scarcely possible to determine the original height of the rock piles, as boulders are somewhat numerous along the lines, perhaps slightly more so than elsewhere: yet, the differences in numbers are so small that we are disposed to conclude that the piles near the bluff could not, on the average, have exceeded fifty centimeters in height. Beyond half the distance out, they seem to have been limited to four or five small boulders each. In no case did we see boulders much larger than the heads of men.

The face of the bluff is perpendicular, a wall of outcropping rock, but at its base is banked up a sharp slope of broken rock, sand and soil. An object falling from the edge would proceed unobstructed for a space of two to three meters, and then striking the sloping surface below, would roll, bounding to the level of the flat.

We visited another site, a few miles down the same stream, which was similar in all essential details. We also received definite descriptions of two other sites on the same reservation by persons familiar with them. On the Blood reserve we saw two sites, one of which was of the type just described. The other, ran the buffalo over a steep hill, apparently the former cutbank of a small near-by creek. We heard of many other sites both on and off the present Blackfoot reserves in Alberta but did not visit them.

At the Two Medicine River site just described, we gathered information from reliable old men as to the manner in which such drives were used. Of course, none of these had seen a drive, but had heard the accounts of their elders time and again. According to these, the herd was run down between the lines of rock piles and forced over the bluff. An enclosure was built below into which the buffalo would fall. Stakes about the size of lodge poles were set in the ground at an angle so that they crossed each other in lattice fashion. This fence was strengthened by binding the crossings of the poles with strips of rawhide. Into this, brush was woven until all the openings were closed. The fence was inclined inward so as to give it greater resistance and also to decrease the probability of the buffalo jumping it. Our informants insisted that no screens of brush were added to the rock lines forming the chute to the enclosure or pound, and that the rock piles were now about as large as when in use. This is contrary to the information furnished Grinnell.[1]

A drive was made by working a bunch of buffalo between the outward ends of the lines. This was done by a few young men on foot, working quietly around a bunch grazing within a few miles of the drive and causing them to

---

[1] Grinnell, (a), 229.

drift toward the lines. This was by no means easy and the failure vere many. The camp was usually on the flat in the vicinity of the drive and a watcher was posted to give notice when a bunch was approaching the chute. When the conditions seemed favorable, he ordered all the young, or able-bodied men, out to the lines where they took their stations behind the rock piles, concealing themselves under blankets or newly cut branches. Then, if the buffalo drifted into the wide entrance to the lines, the outlying men began to stampede them and as they moved forward, the men concealed on their flanks arose shouting, waving blankets or brush, so as to keep them headed down the chute and to increase their fright. When near the brink, the leading buffalo attempted to stop and turn aside. Here, the number of men was greatest and the danger of being run down, considerable; but the pressure of the frightened buffalo in the rear, and the demonstrations of the men near the brink, were usually effective in forcing over the leaders whence the whole bunch followed blindly. The Indians claim that once the buffalo were running in the chute, success was practically assured. The fall maimed some of the buffalo and the others were shot as they milled around in the enclosure. When all were down, the struggling ones were dispatched by striking their foreheads with stone mauls.

In some cases, a swift runner covered with a buffalo robe, hair side out, led the animals down the chute. According to Grinnell, such an individual sometimes unaided, enticed the buffalo into the lines. After horses came into use, the buffalo were sometimes worked into the lines by a few riders, then forced down into the chute by many horsemen on either flank, the lines near the brink being guarded by men on foot as before. The use of the horse, however, and later the gun, caused the drives to fall into disuse, it being much easier to round up a bunch in the open and, riding round and round, shoot them down in rapid succession.

According to some informants, many drives were provided with a middle line of rock piles, much shorter than the others. In such cases two coulees, or depressions led to the brink over the enclosure, the middle line passing along the crest between them. Buffalo running down the main lines might take either of these coulees. The men on this secondary line were directed as to which side to take by a watch posted on a near by knoll. In the diagram, there appears a secondary line outside of the chute, but this is, in reality, a diversion of the main line to cover the mouth of a break in the bluff.

When the driving of buffalo was attempted, many dogs were muzzled to prevent barking. In a piece of tanned hide, a hole was cut large enough to pass over the nose and well up on the jaws. The edges of the piece were drawn back over the head and fastened around the neck with a draw string. By this contrivance, the dog was also hooded. In addition, they were either tied up, yoked to an anchored travois, or weighted with heavy pieces of wood to prevent their finding their way to the pound.

The Piegan positively assert that they never used the Assiniboine, or Cree type, of pound. However, even in recent times, they occasionally made enclosures by pitching tipis closely in a circle and joining the covers. The buffalo were worked into this circle and shot as they stupidly ran round and round.

It will be seen from information secured by us, and the statements of other writers, that the essential features of the buffalo drive among the Piegan and the Blood were an enclosure beneath the brow of a bluff, and irregular lines of rock piles enclosing a V-shaped space. In operation, a few skillful young men worked the buffalo by degrees into the chute formed by these lines, other men then stationed themselves along the lines, then the buffalo were stampeded, the leaders running down between the lines to the brink where they were forced over by their fellows in the rear.[1]

Antelope were taken in a pound somewhat after the method for taking buffalo. There is an old site on Birch Creek in the Blackfoot Reservation, Montana. A pit was dug about two meters wide by six meters long to a depth of from three to four meters. The earth from the excavation was ridged up at the sides of the hole and decked with fresh branches. Two converging lines led up to this pit as in the buffalo pound. There was one important difference, however. As the lines came near together, a turn like an elbow was made to conceal the obstruction at the pit, thus lessening the tendency of the running antelope to jump the line. The lines were marked by small heaps of stones, about a meter apart. Two or more slender willows were bowed over each rock pile, thus forming a kind of fence. When antelope were seen grazing within the lines, the young men stole up to the rear and flanks, while old men, women and even children manned the length of the lines. They lay down behind the rock piles. When the antelope were started and approached a line, the concealed watchers waved something in the air to turn them. Thus, the poor animals ran down between the ever narrowing fences to the brush-covered ridge in front of the pit. Leaping this, they fell into the hole and were caught.[2]

Simple snares were used for deer and smaller game. For deer, a braided rawhide rope was rubbed with buffalo tallow to counteract human odors, then rubbed with white earth, and laid in the trail with an open noose. No bent sapling or trigger was used, the trapper trusting entirely to a chance entanglement of the deer's feet or horns. For catching the weasel, a number of snares were arranged in a small hoop, laid on the hole so that the animal's

---

[1] See also myths, Vol. 2, 27, 85, 109, 112.
[2] Grinnell, (a), 236.

head would be entangled as he came out, the hoop preventing his getting back into the hole. These and other small animals were often snared by hand, the snare operated by a long cord in the hands of a watcher. For birds, small sinew snares were tied to a heavy stick and arranged on the ground with bait.

The wolf, fox and coyote were taken in a kind of deadfall, as their strong teeth sometimes released them from snares. One end of a pole was supported by an upright resting loosely upon a similar horizontal pole lying on the ground. Under the lower end of the upright was thrust the end of the bait stick (Fig. 9). A covering of sticks rested upon the long supported pole and the whole was weighted with stones. As the trap was used only in winter, snow was spread over the top. The bait was a tough piece of meat

Fig. 9. A Deadfall.

from the neck of a buffalo. Usually pieces of paunch or entrails were toasted over the fire, then chewed and the juice spit upon the bait to give it a strong scent. The only part of this trap having a fixed dimension was the supporting upright. For fox, this was cut two hands and two fingers in length (grasping the stick hand over hand). The skins of the fox were stretched over an A-shaped frame for drying. Grinnell says snares were used for these animals and sometimes an enclosure into which they leaped from an incline.[1]

The streams in the region occupied by the Piegan and Blood abound in trout and other fish, which in times of starvation and especially after the buffalo began to disappear, became an important food item. Fish were never speared or shot, but were taken in traps called piskin, the name for buffalo pound. A V-shaped bar of boulders was constructed in the stream, the apex pointing down the current. Such bars were partly of natural for-

---

[1] Grinnell, (a), 240–241.

mation. Logs or poles were laid above this bar and a weir constructed by inclining sticks against them, held in place by strips of willow bark. At the apex of the V, an enclosure of poles was built up cabin-fashion, the interstices being of a size to let the water flow through freely, but to hold the fish. The bar and weir obstructed the current sufficiently to allow this enclosure to be placed below its level, so that the free current fell over into it through a chute.

A simpler but similar method was to weave a kind of basket trap (Fig. 10). This was made of willow twigs about 5 mm. in diameter and a meter in length. This basket had the usual bottle shape seen in fish traps, but its structure was crude, being nothing more than willow rods bound at intervals to hoops of the same material by strands of bark. In operation, weirs were constructed as before, though less elaborate, and the mouth of the basket placed at the apex so that the free current ran through it longi-

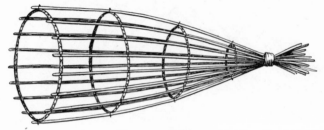

Fig. 10.   A Fish Trap.

tudinally. There was no contrivance to prevent the fish from passing out again at the mouth, but the strength of the current was usually sufficient to force them into the apex of the trap where there was no room to turn. This method was regarded as of ancient origin. Both methods were in use in Montana until prohibited by the State fishing laws.

Eagles were caught by a man concealed in a pit, covered with brush upon which bait was placed. As these birds were taken chiefly for their feathers which were used in ceremonial ways, the art of trapping them was a religious rather than an economic function and hence, not to be discussed at this time.[1]

While it appears, from the foregoing and other data, at our command, that impounding was a dominant method of taking game animals, individual hunting by stalking and otherwise was common. There are many tales of men having run down or otherwise overcome large and powerful animals.

---

[1] See myth, Vol. 2, 135.

For example, a man once crept up to some buffalo, sprang upon the back of one and felled it with a blow from a stone-headed club, his only weapon. However, such tales, if true, only recount athletic feats instead of primitive modes of hunting. The acquisition of horses and guns undoubtedly changed all modes of hunting, and this occurred so long ago that accurate information as to previous practices, is not available.

While the Blackfoot were essentially a hunting people, and game was taken at all times of the year, certain seasons were recognized. Buffalo bulls were regarded in the best condition at about June of our calendar. The cows, on the other hand, were prime "when the leaves began to fall," this being, in recent times, the great hunting season. The time for fishing was in the spring of the year "when the night hawks first began to call."

The man did most of the butchering, but when the meat was brought home it became at once the property of the women in his family. When game was killed near the camp, the women took a hand in the butchering, but usually under the active direction of the men. There was, however, no disgrace for women to engage in butchering:— as with us, dish-washing is woman's work, though some men may safely do it, so with the Blackfoot, butchering was man's work, though some women did it.

Buffalo were not bled, though when shot back of the shoulder they bled profusely at the mouth. Buffalo or other animals were improved by running before killing. In dressing, the skin was cut down the median line of the breast and worked loose. Then the carcass as it lay on the outstretched skin was disemboweled. The manner of its dismemberment depended on the distance from camp. Assuming that the carcass was in camp, the procedure for buffalo or deer was about as follows:— The fore quarters were removed by cutting down through the shoulder joints. Then cuts were made at the shins. The hind legs were cut off and the quarters cut at the hip joints. The back-fat was removed in broad bands. The breast and belly were cut away in one piece; then the short ribs, eight on a side, in two pieces; also two similar pieces of neck ribs. The parts of the loin containing the kidneys were taken next. The "boss ribs" (hump) were stripped. If there was a feotus it was tied up with the "boss ribs." [1] The back bone was cut into two pieces. A chunk of meat from the rump and one from the neck were taken. The heart, tongue, brain, paunch and small intestines were taken. Sometimes the hoofs and some of the head meat were also taken. The marrow from the leg bones was usually eaten raw during the butchering. While, at the present time cattle are butchered in this way, the scarcity of food compels the Indian to use every part of the carcass.

---

[1] The Canadian name for the spinous process in the hump, Franklin, 102.

In former times, when hunting on horses, it was necessary to prepare the carcass for packing. If the camp was near by, the procedure was about as stated above. The fresh skin was laid on the horse's back, the head piece toward his head. A strip of the hide was slipped through under the tendons of the fore quarters so they could be hung across the horse. The hind quarters were tied together by their own tendons and treated in a similar manner. The short ribs and the large pieces from the breast and belly were rolled up. The neck ribs, heart, tongue, back-fat, etc., were made up into bundles and placed on the horse. The tail end of the skin was then turned up over the pack of meat. This method was spoken of as "heavy butchering."

"Light butchering" was the term applied to a method much used when the killing was far from camp or when several animals were to be transported by one or two horses. In this case, the loins were cut out of the quarters. Then these were tied in pairs as before. The back-fat was removed in two pieces, and tied so as to lay across the horse. The loins with the kidneys, the meat from the boss ribs, the heart, the tongue, breast and groin were taken as before. The flesh over the ribs was worked off in one piece. The paunch was emptied and the small intestines stripped. The whole was then packed in the skin on a horse as for the "heavy butchering." Thus, the bones were left behind. The marrow and sometimes the brain were eaten as the butchering went on.[1]

The only tool used in butchering was a heavy metal knife. The bone of the fore leg was often used as a club to break smaller bones and joints. The time required for cutting up a carcass was short, as men now living claim to have been able unaided to butcher from five to twelve buffalo in a day. We have no way of knowing how butchering was carried on before the advent of metal knives, but the fact noted elsewhere, that occasionally in recent times butchering was, by necessity, done with stone flakes, suggests· the probability of its accomplishment by these methods without steel knives.

Comparative Notes. There seems to be little that can be considered distinctive in the food preferences of the Blackfoot. In the choice of vegetable foods they agree with most of the roving tribes in the Missouri-Saskatchewan Basin.[2] The Sarcee, Plains Cree, Assiniboine, Gros Ventre, Teton, Yankton, Crow and Cheyenne, at least, made similar use of wild turnips, wild cherries and plums. The use of these and other vegetables naturally depended upon the distribution of the various species. This is quite obvious in case of the camas, an important food plant in the valley of the Columbia and the interior plateaus northward.[3] This plant grows among

---

[1] For comparison see Harmon 286.

[2] For use of this term see American Anthropologist, p. 197, Vol. 10, No. 2.

[3] Palmer, 408.

the foothills on the east of the Rocky Mountains adjacent to the territory of the Blackfoot, where it is gathered and prepared after the method used by the Nez Percé,[1] Flathead and other plateau tribes. In this case, there can be little doubt that the practice is due to Blackfoot contact with plateau culture. When we consider the fact that they are also on the northwestern edge of the habitat of the prairie turnip, a very popular food among the Siouan groups, it becomes probable that even this was due to cultural contact. Wild rice seems not to have come within their experience, nor is there any evidence of the use of wild grains, as among the northern Shoshone. The use of berries, however, seems to have been considerable, and in this respect, they resemble the Thompson,[2] Carrier[3] and other tribes of the interior plateaus. Yet even these tribes made use of roots in great variety and quantity in contrast to the Blackfoot. The northern Shoshone[4] show certain similarities to the plateau tribes in the range and quantity of vegetable food, but in addition make use of seeds, or grains, something of which the Blackfoot seem to have no traditional knowledge. Information on the vegetable foods of the Crow is not available for comparison.

The fact, that the vegetable food of the Blackfoot seems to have been normally used as the secondary element in meat dishes, leaves little to be said as to cooking and preparation. The detail of the method used in cooking camas does not essentially differ from that used by the Thompson Indians for dry roots of all kinds.[5] In brief, this method of cooking roots in a hole seems to be generally distributed in the interior plateau and adjacent coast areas.[6] In the drying of berries, the Blackfoot do not follow the practices of the plateau tribes who usually reduce all berries to a mash which is cooked somewhat before drying. The Carriers for example, used an ingenious device by which the mashing and cooking was somewhat automatic.[7] Yet, so far as our information goes, the Blackfoot dried the service and other berries without mashing or cooking, the mash being used for cherries only and then chiefly in the manufacture of pemmican. In this respect, they resemble their southeastern neighbors.

In the matter of animal food, the Blackfoot naturally belong to the Missouri-Saskatchewan type, the buffalo and animals of the deer-kind furnishing the main support of life. While the disposition of the Blackfoot to refuse fish can scarcely be taken as characteristic of the area, positive inform-

---

[1] Spinden, (b), 201.
[2] Teit, 230.
[3] Morice, (a), 216.
[4] Lowie, 187.
[5] Teit, 236.
[6] Hill-Tout, 101.
[7] Morice, (a), 217.

ation for most tribes is wanting. The Gros Ventre did not make much use of them.[1]   In the south, the Navaho and the Apache, tabooed fish, while among the Dakota and Cree they sometimes formed a considerable part of their winter food, though apparently from necessity rather than choice.   As practically none of the buffalo-eating tribes touched the salmon area, the disinclination to use fish may be due to economic conditions.   While many tribes eat the flesh of the dog, the Blackfoot show a special antipathy toward it.   According to Clark [2] the Crow, Flathead, Nez Perce, Snake, Bannock and Ute did not eat dog; but among the Dakota, Arapaho, Kiowa, Apache and Pawnee, they were regarded as a delicacy.   This seems to indicate a geographical distribution of the custom, rather than a linguistic one, the Blackfoot falling in the northwestern cultural group.

It may be, that a ceremonial has been one of the chief factors in the distribution of this custom.   Among the Pawnee, a dog was usually served at ceremonial feasts and it appears that among the Dakota its serving was a prominent feature of many dances. · The so-called Omaha Dance is now the great occasion of a Dakota dog feast.   The Gros Ventre have this dance and its dog feast.   The Piegan learned it of the Gros Ventre and make some effort to eat dog-soup at the time of the ceremony.[3]   At least, there is a tendency for this ceremony to introduce the custom among the Blackfoot.

In the manufacture of pemmican, the Blackfoot followed the general type of the plains.   Harmon states that the tribes east of the Rocky Mountains in Canada, pound up wild cherries in the manner described.[4]   Nuttal speaks of a similar general distribution for the central and southern plains area.[5]   Franchère notes the same kind of pemmican in the Columbia region. In most cases, this food was stored in a folded rawhide, generally called a parfleche.   While the buffalo-chasing tribes seem to have been the centre of the berry-pemmican industry, the more general type of pemmican; i. e., unmixed pounded meat, was widely known among the Athapascan and Algonkin peoples.   To the west of the Rocky Mountains in the salmon country, pulverized dried fish was a common food.   Thus, we have a wide distribution of the method of pulverizing, or grinding, dried meat by the mortar process.

Information as to the methods of cooking meats is not abundant for the neighbors of the Blackfoot.   In a general way, the American tribes in con-

---

[1] Kroeber, (a), 149.

[2] Clark, 154.

[3] Dr. Lowie reports the Stoney Assiniboine as refusing dog in contrast to the other Assiniboine and curiously enough makes no mention of this ceremony among the Stoney but reports it at length for the Ft. Belknap division.   This is in harmony with the above.   P. 67, Vol. 4, this series.

[4] Harmon, 282.

[5] Nuttal, 194.

trast to the Ocianians, were great pot boilers. In regions where pottery or stone vessels were not in use, boiling was in baskets or wooden vessels by means of hot stones. So far, the use of pottery vessels has not been fully proven for the Assiniboine, Gros Ventre, Sarcee, Blackfoot, Crow, Arapaho, Kiowa, Comanche and Cheyenne. Some of these have traditions of pottery, more or less probable, but definite statements by explorers are wanting, leaving the case, as tentative.[1]

So far, there has come to our notice no mention of cooking meat in an earth-covered hole as described by the Blackfoot. Swan [2] saw birds cooked with hot stones after the same general mode. However, the distribution of a similar method for cooking vegetables in the plateau area again suggests Blackfoot cultural contact with their western neighbors.

The use of a paunch or skin vessel for boiling was known to the Arapaho [3] and the Crow.[4] The Gros Ventre, near neighbors to the Blackfoot used "rawhide bags, drawn together at the top with a string" and "holes in the ground lined with rawhide." [5] From the Teton Dakota, the writer obtained a full description agreeing in all essential details with the method among the Blackfoot.[6] Here also, it was used chiefly by war parties. Mr. Skinner reports a similar practice by hunting parties among the Eastern Cree though the vessel is hung directly over the source of heat. The Haidatsa seem to have had the same custom.[7] The Assiniboine method of cooking in a hole has been described by Catlin as follows:—

"There is a very curious custom amongst the Assinneboins, from which they have taken their name; a name given them by their neighbors, from a singular mode they have of boiling their meat, which is done in the following manner:— when they kill meat, a hole is dug in the ground about the size of a common pot, and a piece of the raw hide of the animal, as taken from the back, is put over the hole, and then pressed down with the hands close around the sides, and filled with water. The meat to be boiled is then put in this hole or pot of water; and in a fire which is built near by, several large stones are heated to a red heat, which are successively dipped and held in the water until the meat is boiled; from which singular and peculiar custom, the Ojibeways have given them the appellation of Assinneboins or stone boilers.

"The Traders have recently supplied these people with pots; and even long before that, the Mandans had instructed them in the secret of manufacturing very good and serviceable earthen pots; which together have entirely done away the custom, excepting at public festivals; where they seem, like all others of the human family, to take pleasure in cherishing and perpetuating their ancient customs."

1 Mooney, 18.
2 Swan, 271.
3 Kroeber, (b), 25.
4 Curtis, 4.
5 Kroeber, (a), 150.
6 See also Schoolcraft, (b) part 2, 176.
7 Matthews, 23.

Turning to the westward, we find that the Thompson Indians when out on the hunt sometimes resorted to the use of bark kettles or a deer's paunch. "A hole was dug in the soft ground near the fire, into which the kettle was placed, with brush underneath. The open end was made small and stiff by means of a stick threaded through it around the edge; and the sides of the open end were sometimes fastened with bark to one or two cross-sticks which lay on the ground across the opening. Hot stones were put in to boil the food." [1]   The more general practice of stone boiling is a well known cultural trait of the whole Pacific Coast and interior plateaus from southern California to Alaska and parts of the Mackenzie Basin and eastward. Tylor has given a comprehensive statement of its distribution. [2]   Noting that the Blackfoot in particular, and many other buffalo hunting tribes in general, lay as a wedge between the stone boiling and the pot boiling areas, it may be expected that, since traces of pottery are meager, they will show decided tendencies to adopt the practice of stone boiling.. True to their environment and non-basket making habits, they used skins and paunch in contrast to the bark vessels of the northeast and the baskets of the southwest. To return to the Blackfoot, we find them in no way peculiar in this respect, having at least the boiling characteristics of their neighbors and the Dakota. In how far this boiling in·skins may have once been a general household practice is a matter of conjecture rather than otherwise. It is natural to assume that its practice by war parties and other travelers is in the nature of a survival, but it remains an assumption. In its more modern form, at least among the Thompson, Cree, Assiniboine [3] and Blackfoot Indians, it was limited to hunting and war parties, and in consequence was nearly always performed by men. The distribution of this peculiar type of man's cooking can scarcely be accounted for as independent in origin, but must have resulted from tribal contact.

In the materials for culinary utensils there is great uniformity in America. Horn, wood and bark were used for bowls and spoons from the Gulf of Mexico to Alaska, though apparently to a less degree in California and the Colorado-Rio Grande Area. In the eastern and central Algonkin areas, however, the wooden spoon seems to have been the prevailing type, occurring even in the interior of Labrador. [4]   Carver [5] states that wooden spoons were used in the countries visited by him but makes no mention of horn spoons. We have seen buffalo horn spoons from the Gros Ventre and the Assiniboine without handles or with mere tips. This is similar to the usual modern

[1] Teit, 246.
[2] Tylor, 264.
[3] This series, p. 12, Vol. 4.
[4] Turner, 302.
[5] Carver, 234.

form of Blackfoot big-horn spoons, or dippers. The horn spoons of the Dakota seen by us have graceful shapes and long handles, the ends of which terminate in an enlarged head. This head and the adjoining part of the handle is often carved to represent a snake. Among the Dakota, we also find wooden spoons, one very old specimen seen by us being shaped like the medium sized big-horn spoons. In a general way, it appears that the spoons of the Gros Ventre and Blackfoot are about equally crude when compared to those of the Dakota. Information and material for further comparison within the Missouri-Saskatchewan area is not accessible to us.

The use of knots in the manufacture of wooden bowls was not peculiar to the Blackfoot. According to information collected by the writer, they were made by the Dakota by methods similar to those employed by the Blackfoot.[1] Long states that "as we were cutting up a log an Indian saw a knot and asked for it to make a bowl. He called a woman to cut it off for him." [2] From the specimens at our command, it appears that the wooden bowls of the Siouan tribes excelled those of other parts of the continent in lightness and perfection of form. While we have seen specimens from the Sauk and Fox and Menominee approximating the graceful shapes of the Dakota, they were much heavier and less symmetrical. Wooden bowls are rare in the collections we have seen from the Shoshone, Ute and Comanche and when they do occur, are inclined to be heavy and crude.

Vessels made of skin seem to have been in use among tribes to the east and south of the Blackfoot. We have seen a pail from the Gros Ventre made of a cow's bladder. The Museum collection from the Haidatsa Indians has two water pails of buffalo paunch and one of peracardium. Long describes water vessels made of paunch, observed among the Kaskaia and other tribes.[3] Lewis and Clark say of the Teton, "the water which they carry with them is contained chiefly in the paunch of deer and other animals."[4] Henry saw among the Assiniboine "an ox's (buffalo's) paunch employed as a kettle, for melting snow." [5] Thus there seems nothing distinctive of the Blackfoot in these particulars.

Fortunately for our purpose, the methods of killing buffalo have been described by several writers. The most satisfactory general review seems to be by J. A. Allen in his famous memoir on the American bisons. From this review it appears that during the historic period, the Indians followed four distinct co-operative methods, driving over cliffs, impounding, grass-firing and surrounding. Other methods such as chasing on snow shoes, on

[1] Lewis and Clark, 140; Carver, 234.
[2] James, 1, 166.
[3] James, 2, 295.
[4] Lewis and Clark, 1, 140.
[5] Henry, 291.

the ice, in the water, stalking etc., may be successfully pursued by single individuals acting independently and without organization. We shall pass over these methods and give our attention to the distribution of the co-operative methods. The use of the pound, as noted among the Northern Blackfoot seems to have been characteristic of the Assiniboine. The earliest definite account of this method noted by us, is by the elder Henry [1] as observed by him in 1776. The younger Henry [2] also writes, apparently from observation, in 1809. Father de Smet writing in 1854 describes an Assiniboine drive as witnessed by himself.[3] These observers are in general agreement as to the structure of the pound. The enclosure was circular, built of trees, brush, stones, and stakes to the height of five or six feet. It was placed in a narrow valley between two hills, or rather at the point where two converging ranges of low hills met and usually in a clump of trees. An inclined plane, or slope, led up to the top of the enclosure. The lines near the pound were formed of materials similar to the walls just described. At a distance of about one hundred meters they gradually break into an open line of sticks. The lines are about two miles in length. The buffalo were worked into the lines by two or three men, imitating the sound of a calf in distress,[4] by setting fire to grass,[5] etc., each man doubtless using his own method. Once near the lines guarded by men, the buffalo were led along by a swift runner or horseman covered with buffalo robes, and frightened by the men in the lines are forced into the pound. Franklin also saw an Assiniboine pound and notes that a tree stood in the middle on which offerings were placed.[6]

The Plains Cree seem to have followed the same method. There were, however, some slight differences in the pound, as a palisaded enclosure and a ditch or pit (?) to prevent escape by the entrance. Also, their pound did not always have an inclined plane by which the buffalo could enter, the opening being on the level and guarded by skins held by poles or even by persons. This account of Hind's [7] is criticised by Hector and Vaux in a manner that leads one to suspect the Cree used the precise method of the Assiniboine. This is confirmed by a description of a Cree pound by John McDougall.[8] Henry makes the statement that pounds were used by the Assiniboine in winter but not in summer.[9] Hector and Vaux also specifically deny Hind's statement that they were used in summer. Also, it was winter when the

[1] Henry, 294.
[2] Henry and Thompson, 518.
[3] De Smet, 1027.
[4] De Smet, 1030.
[5] Henry and Thompson, 577.
[6] Franklin, 101.
[7] Hind, 357.
[8] McDougall, 273.
[9] Henry and Thompson, 518.

elder Henry made his observation and curiously enough the visit of the younger Henry to a Blackfoot pound was in December. Maximilian says the Blackfoot made pounds in winter.[1] While pounds of this type were doubtless used at all times of the year before horses were introduced, the presence of these animals made a resort to this method unnecessary in summer. The tendency among all observers was to consider impounding the primitive mode.

Illustrations of pounds may be found in the works of Umfreville, Hind, and Franklin. The former, gives a general description apparently not referring to any particular tribe; he states, however, that the enclosures are circular or square, according to the nation using them. Harmon[2] mentions having seen pounds in use and gives a description of them agreeing in many particulars with that of Umfreville. So far, the Assiniboine type has been found in use among the Plains Cree and Northern Blackfoot. The younger Henry states that the Assiniboine were usually considered "the most expert and dexterous nation of the plains in constructing pounds, and in driving buffalo into them."[3] Maximilian makes a similar statement.[4] These taken with the limited distribution of this type of pound suggest strongly the Assiniboine as the centre of distribution.

The use of a cliff or cut-bank over which the buffalo fell into a pound might be assumed a makeshift to avoid the construction of the incline. However, the enclosure was not always present. Schoolcraft[5] says "the bands inhabiting the Missouri" drive buffalo over precipices. According to Allen,[6] this was the practice of the Minnetarees, though Lewis[7] in his description refers the practice to the "Indians of the Missouri." The first of these drives noted by Lewis and Clark was, however, near the mouth of the Judith River, in territory in which he expected to meet the Gros Ventre and Blackfoot tribes. In 1873 Allen[8] saw remains of a pound "above the mouth of the Big Horn River" which from the context appears to have been of the Blackfoot type. Hornaday[9] quotes T. R. Davis as stating that the Indians between the Platte and Arkansas Rivers were seen by him driving buffaloes over ledges.[10] From notes by Kroeber,[11] the Gros Ventre seem to

---

[1] Maximilian, 252.
[2] Harmon, 285.
[3] Henry and Thompson, 518.
[4] Maximilian, 195.
[5] Schoolcraft, 279.
[6] Allen, 204.
[7] Lewis and Clark, 2, 93.
[8] Allen, 207.
[9] Hornaday, 483.

[10] The following extract from a letter by Mr. Reese Kincaide is given in confirmation:—
"In talking to Washee, one of the Arapaho chiefs, about this matter, he said that he remembers seeing the Arapaho hunters drive a herd of buffalo over a bluff in Colorado. The dead lay in a great pile and as the weather was very cold the bodies froze, so that the women worked for several weeks curing the meat and hides. George Bent, a Cheyenne, says that in the winter of 1872, he saw the Indians drive a bunch of buffalo over a bluff on the Cimarron River of Oklahoma and that many were killed. These likewise froze, so the women could take their time in saving the meat and hides. As to driving them into pens, I could find nothing."

[11] Kroeber, (a), 148.

have followed the methods of the Piegan and Blood. Henry [1] saw in the Rocky Mountains a precipice over which the Kootenai drove buffalo and perhaps other animals.

According to Allen,[2] rounding up buffalo by firing the grass was noted by Hennepin, Du Pratz, Charlevoix and J. G. Shea. To these may be added Schoolcraft [3] and Carver.[4] Schoolcraft states that the method by fire was used on the upper Mississippi. From all these accounts, it appears that this method was chiefly in vogue in the prairies of Wisconsin, Illinois, Iowa and Minnesota, and therefore practised by the Algonkin and Siouan tribes within these limits.

The surround was evidently a method developed after the introduction of the horse. A large body of horsemen under the direction of leaders rode round and round a flying herd, shooting down the animals as they rushed about. Descriptions of this have been given by Catlin,[5] James,[6] Grinnell,[7] and others. It appears that at the opening of the period this method was common to the Minnetarees,[8] Mandan,[9] Arikara,[10] Pawnee,[11] Arapaho,[11] Omaha,[11] Cheyenne [11] and the southern tribes generally. Later, it was used in summer by all the northern tribes.

Now, while the information at our command is not entirely adequate for the purpose, the general distribution of the types of co-operative buffalo hunting and the place of the Blackfoot in this culture area can be stated with considerable confidence. The pound of the Assiniboine was used by the Plains Cree and the Northern Blackfoot. According to Grinnell,[12] the Cheyenne at one time used a similar pound, which, taken with the fact that this tribe once lived on the borders of the Cree-Assiniboine area, is suggestive. Driving over a cliff or a ledge with or without an enclosure below was largely practised by the Piegan, Blood, Gros Ventre, Kootenai and probably by the Haidatsa and Crow. The method of surrounding by fire was used by the Santee division of the Dakota, the Algonkin of the upper Mississippi valley and probably the Iowa and Winnebago. Rounding up, by horsemen was the prevailing mode of the Arapaho, Cheyenne, Mandan and southern Siouan tribes, the Caddoan tribes and perhaps some of the

---

[1] Henry and Thompson, 691.
[2] Allen, 202.
[3] Schoolcraft, (a) 279.
[4] Carver, 287.
[5] Catlin, 1, 199.
[6] James, 1, 190.
[7] Grinnell, (b), 284.
[8] Catlin, 1, 199.
[9] Spinden and Will, 121.
[10] Brackenridge, 157.
[11] Hornaday, 483.
[12] Grinnell, (a), 231.

Shoshonian tribes. Thus, the Blackfoot seem to be territorially divided between two types, the pound and the drive over a cliff. There may be some justification in regarding these as varieties of the same type since they prevailed in contiguous parts of the Saskatchewan and Upper Missouri country. Harmon states that the pounds observed by him (the Assiniboine type) were placed in a clump of trees with the opening facing "a rising piece of ground, that the yard (enclosure) may not be seen from a distance." [1] Thus the Piegan and Blood type may be a normal variation from that of the Assiniboine.

The method by firing the grass can scarcely be considered as a variant of this general impounding type, even though fire was often employed to work the buffalo into the lines of a pound. Both, however, may be considered as distinct from the "surround" in that horses were not necessary to them but absolutely essential to the latter. To quote from Schoolcraft:— "The Indians employ both the rifle and the arrow, and in the prairies of Missouri and Arkansas, pursue the herds on horseback; but on the upper Mississippi, where they are destitute of horses, they make amends for this deficiency by several ingenious stratagems. One of the most common of these is the method of hunting with fire." [2] We have previously pointed out the tendency of the northern tribes to use pounds in winter and not in summer. As the horse was evidently gradually introduced from the southwest, the inference is that impounding and grass-firing were methods being displaced by the surround in the course of events. However this may be, the Blackfoot seem to fall into a group with the Assiniboine, Plains Cree, Gros Ventre, Kootenai, and possibly the Crow and Haidatsa.

The antelope pound used by the Blackfoot is quite similar to a description secured from the Teton except that the lines were not provided with the elbow-like turn and terminated in an enclosure instead of a pit. It seems that the Mandan used a form like that of the Teton. (It is strange that no reference to their using a buffalo pound is found). Grinnell saw the ruins of antelope pounds "in northwestern Utah, in the country ranged over by the Utes, Cheyennes and Arapahoes." [3] According to Charlevoix some such impounding was used in Canada for moose, caribou and deer.[4] Lewis[5] saw an antelope pound used by the Assiniboine similar to that of the Teton. According to the same writer the Shoshone use a form of the surround for taking antelope.[6] De Smet [7] gives a general description of antelope pounds

---

[1] Harmon, 286.
[2] Schoolcraft, (a) 279.
[3] Grinnell, (c) 60.
[4] Allen, 207.
[5] Lewis and Clark, 1, 313.
[6] Lewis and Clark, 2, 345.
[7] De Smet, 1397.

similar to those of the Teton. It seems that the Blackfoot show some individuality in the use of the pit and the elbowed lines. The Coeur D'Alene used a form of grass-firing for deer.[1]

The Blackfoot, like their immediate neighbors, were not given to the taking of fur-bearing animals. The traps used by them were few and simple, and looked upon as pertaining to boyish things. It may be of interest to note that the general form of deadfall herein described was rather widely distributed in North America. The form of fish trap (Fig. 10) is similar to that used by the Haidatsa, but whatever its origin it is certainly intrusive.

In conclusion, it must be said that we have found little in the preceding that seemed truly characteristic of the Blackfoot. All their food habits seem to have been shared almost equally by the tribes of the Saskatchewan and the Upper Missouri. In a few methods of cooking, they show similarities to parts of the western plateau area and may, perhaps, be credited with slight individuality in the forms of some utensils.

---

[1] De Smet, 1021.

Manufactures.

In all considerations of material culture, the productive processes of the home, and indeed there are few that are not of the home, must receive a great deal of attention. To be consistent, of course, all the objects described in this paper should be considered specimens of domestic production; but for convenience sake, we have chosen this head for the study of such as do not readily find their places elsewhere, or in which the process is of more importance to our problems than the functions of the resulting objects.

Textile Arts. Like most peoples of the Missouri-Saskatchewan area, the Blackfoot gave little attention to textiles, skins sufficing for their needs. No traces of basketry could be found. Soft woven bags from across the

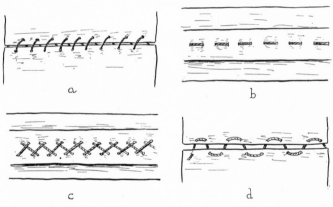

Fig. 11.   Stitches used in Sewing.

mountains are in use, but none were made by the Blackfoot themselves. A crude kind of fish trap has been described and some forms of the sweat house may be interpreted as attempts at basketry, but these few exceptions seem, after all, to prove the rule. As to weaving, the wrapped technique in dog travois frames is the sole instance.

Formerly, cord was made from the tough bark of an unidentified shrub (the buffalo berry?) which was twisted or plaited into ropes, doubtless similar to the hair and thong ropes described elsewhere. Thread for sewing was of sinew. Large broad bands of sinew from the legs and neck of a steer are dried and stored. When thread is needed some shreds are pulled off by the teeth, softened in water or in the mouth and smoothed out with the fingers. Then placing one end in the mouth, the shreds are twisted by rolling between the palms. Sometimes the end is held under the foot. Heavy cord, or even rope, is occasionally made by twisting or braiding similar strands of twisted thread. (Plate ii.)

For sewing, a bodkin of bone was used. This was displaced by those of metal and finally, in time, by needles. Their chief stitches are shown in Fig. 11. The first of these is the one in general use for all seams and the joining of moccasin soles to their uppers, often spoken of as over and over stitch. The second is in our terminology the running stitch of plain sewing,

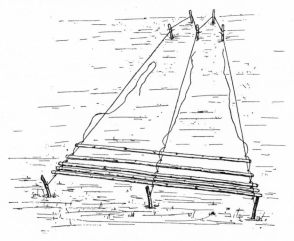

Fig. 12.   Frame for a Back Rest.

used by the Blackfoot for attaching borders and bands. The third is used as a mending stitch, while the fourth is chiefly for ornament. While these are very simple, they were primarily devised for work in skins and should be judged from that point of view. It appears that the use of two threads, as in our shoe and leather work, is unknown. We have not found time to examine many specimens from other tribes, but find the first and third in general use so far as our observation goes.[1]

Back rests, used in tipis at the heads of couches, may perhaps be considered as examples of weaving. They are made of willows tied with sinew. As a rule, they are held together by three strands of cord. First, three cords,

---

[1] The stitches were determined by Miss R. B. Howe.

the proper length for a rest, are tightly stretched on stakes (Fig. 12). Those at the base are driven in firmly: those at the other extremity are reinforced by cords attached to two other stakes.[1] The willows are then laid on, beginning at the base. Around each stretched cord is passed another as in Fig. 13, and drawn tight, thus securely tying each rod to its neighbor and the warp cord. While in most cases, the loose cord is introduced as shown in the figure, it is occasionally tied in a true knot. In most back rests, the willows are also perforated and strung with two strands of sinew. The reason for this is not quite clear. Some Cheyenne rests in the Museum are held together

Fig. 13.   The Back Rest Stitch.

entirely by stringing, suggesting that the Blackfoot may have combined two techniques in the making of one object.

Technique of Bead and Quill Work. The use of quills in ornamentation has almost become a thing of the past; hence, few specimens came to our notice. On the other hand, we have the testimony of many early observers to the effect that formerly these people were very efficient in this art. However, we collected specimens of the following technique, the details of which were determined by Mr. William C. Orchard. For convenience, we have given each a serial number.

1. In this technique, the quills are laid on in rows or bands. Designs are worked out by changing the color of the quills. The ends of the quills

Fig. 14.   Quill Technique No. 1.

Fig. 15.   Technique No. 3.

on the lower edge of a band are held in place by a string of sinew, or thread, *a,* running across the surface of the leather to be decorated, with another thread, *b,* going in the same direction but passing under the first thread through the surface of the leather, back over the first thread and under itself, thus forming a loop between each quill (Fig. 14). The thread holding the

---

[1] In use heavy pieces of wood or other weights are laid upon these cords to regulate the tension of the strands, or warps. For back rests in use see, Plate VII.

upper end of the quills in place, is threaded through the surface of the leather in an oblique direction, from left to right (assuming that the work is started from the right hand side) crossing under itself on to the next space between the quills. This is practically the same stitch as that employed for the lower edge, omitting thread *a* (50–4452–5452).

2. This is done with a simple stitch, the thread caught under the surface of the leather between each turn of the quill (Fig. 16). Patterns are produced by varying the lengths of the quills (50–5377, 76).

3. In this process (Fig. 15) the surface is similar to that for No. 1 but

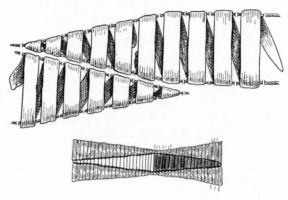

Fig. 16.   Technique No. 2.

the stitch is simple. The thread is passed through the leather and back again between each quill (50–6787).

4. This gives a diagonal effect and is laid on in narrow bands (Fig. 17). The quills are held in place by a loop stitch as described for No. 1 (50–5427).

Fig. 17.   Technique No. 4.

5. In this form of decoration, the quill crosses itself obliquely producing a V-shaped surface pattern. To get this effect, the end of the quill is held under the stitch, turned back on itself over the stitch, to the opposite edge of

the band where a parallel stitch is made over the quill, which is again turned
back to the opposite side where another stitch is made, etc., Fig. 18 (50–6164).

6. The method employed in this case may be termed a plaiting, where
two elements are active, crossing each other obliquely, under one and over
one, which is practically a weave, forming a diamond shaped pattern. The
quills are held in position by a thread laid over them at such places where it
will be covered by the next crossing quill, or as in the case of the edge, where
the quill turns back over itself. The thread is caught under the surface of

Fig. 19.

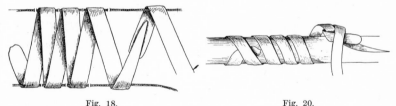

Fig. 18.					Fig. 20.

Fig. 18.	Technique No. 5.
Fig. 19.	Technique No. 6.
Fig. 20.	Technique No. 7.

the leather at the interstices, the direction of which is shown in the dotted
lines in Fig. 19. This form of quill work may be used for narrow bands, or
in widths limited only by the size of the article to be decorated. Where
the width is more than the length of a quill, a system of lapping is used.
When the length of a quill is used, the end is caught under a stitch in the
nearest row, the end of another tucked under the same stitch and turned
back over itself, whence the plaiting proceeds. The lappings are all carefully concealed under the crossing elements (50–7422, 4484).

7.   A different kind of technique (Fig. 20) is often used on a leather base for the lacings of moccasins, fringes or bands.   The end of the quill is over-lapped and the winding proceeded with until the extremity of the quill is reached around which the end of another quill is turned half around and overlapped by the next layer.   The lappings are arranged so that they always occur on the same side.   The end is turned back under the last laps at the finish (50–5377, 76).

8.   This is used chiefly on a kind of fringe with a rawhide strip as a base, around which quills are twined and held in place by a thread, running the length of the strip, each extremity passing through from one side and knotted on the other.   One end of the quill is passed under the thread; the remaining portion is turned back and overlaps the end, and then twined around the strip two or three times, according to the length of the quill and width of the strip until the other end is reached, which is turned over and tucked under the thread to complete the binding.   Other quills are added in like manner

Fig. 21.   Technique No. 8.   Fig. 22.   Technique No. 9.

until the entire length of the strip is covered.   The side on which the thread shows is the back and all beginnings and endings are made there.   The edges of the quills are spread apart in the drawing to show the method, Fig. 21 (50–4452).

In all quill work where thread is used and the quills appear on one side only, the stitches pass in and out on the same side of the leather, thus not to be seen on the reverse side.   This may be taken as characteristic of all quill work so far observed in our collections.   Of the preceding techniques all were certainly extensively used by the Blackfoot with the possible exception of the last.   This we suspect was recently learned from some of their neighbors as the pipe bag upon which it usually occurs is not typical.   In the case of No. 1 it is not clear why a different stitch is used on each edge of the band as we have no data from the workers themselves.   The women kept quills of assorted colors in cigar shaped bags of gut.   When at work, the quills were held in the mouth to soften, flattened and made flexible by working with the fingers and immediately put into place.

We are able to present some comparative observations on the technique of neighboring tribes as determined by Mr. Orchard.

9. A technique found on some Gros Ventre specimens is shown in Fig. 22. The stitch along the upper edge is made by looping the thread through the surface of the leather between each quill, that on the lower edge is caught through the surface in an oblique direction omitting the loop which in sewing technique is known as a "back stitch" (50–4262).

10. In this method of sewing quills to leather, a single thread is employed around which the quill is turned, the thread being caught through the surface of the leather between each turn of the quill (Fig. 23). The stitch is hidden behind that part of the quill forming a loop in front. It is used for single

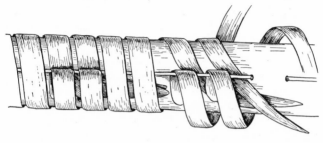

Fig. 24.

Fig. 23.

Fig. 25.

Fig. 23.   Technique No. 10.
Fig. 24.   Technique No. 11.
Fig. 25.   Technique No. 12.

lines and edgings in designs and so far observed among the Gros Ventre and on an unidentified specimen in the Audubon collection (50–4275).

11. The following is another method of fastening quills to a lace or other object to be decorated:— A thread is passed through the lace from one side to the other and knotted. The root ends of one or two quills are placed side by side, the quills are turned back over their ends and wrapped around the lace until the points are reached. The points are turned down the lace at right angles to the wrapping, and under the thread, which is passed through the leather, immediately below the turning of the quills. The thread is pulled tight, holding the quills securely (Fig. 24). To continue

the wrapping, two more quill ends are tucked under the thread immediately over the turning point of the preceding quills, turned back and wrapped as before, until the lace is covered. It was observed among the Gros Ventre (50–4312).

12. The Gros Ventre also have a simple winding for laces. The root end of the quill is overlapped and the winding proceeded with until the point is reached which is turned down and overlapped by the succeeding quill with the root and treated as at the starting point. For the finish, the point is turned back under the last laps (Fig. 25). (50–1789.)

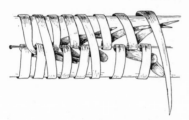

Fig. 26.   Technique No. 13.

13. A method of winding quills on a narrow band observed among the Assiniboine and the Gros Ventre is as follows:— A thread is stretched along the surface, down the middle of a strip of rawhide, and secured at the extremities by passing the thread through perforations and knotting on the reverse side. The end of a quill is tucked under a string so stretched, the quill turned back over its end and around the strip where the point is carried beyond the thread turned down and tucked under. Another quill is started as in the first place and the

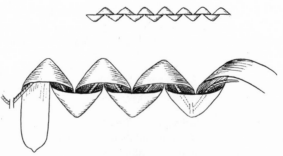

Fig. 27.   Technique No. 14.

operation repeated until the strip is covered (Fig. 26). The ends and points are all turned down along the thread toward the end of the strip until the last ends are reached, which are turned up and tucked under the preceding laps to form a finish. In some places, two laps are made by the quill but in the majority, only one. The accumulations of points and ends form a very decided ridge along the centre of the strip (50–1935, 4308, 7423).

14.   In this form of decoration, the sinew is made to run through upper and lower loops in the leather, and the quill twisted around the sinew between each stitch and turned at an angle to make another turn around the

Fig. 28.   Technique No. 15.

next stitch.   The sinew is caught under the surface of the leather beneath the apex of each sharp turn (Fig. 27).   It was observed in an unidentified specimen in the Audubon collection.

15.   Among the Assiniboine and also in the Audubon collection occurs a narrow band plaiting similar to No. 14, Fig. 28 (50–2003).

16.   Another form of quill bound strips of soft leather occurs among the Assiniboine (Fig. 29).   A knotted string is passed through the leather and turned down over the end of a quill which is turned back over itself, wound around the leather strip until the point is reached, which is turned down under the thread

Fig. 29.   Technique No. 16.

where another quill end is inserted and turned back over itself and around the strip, and so on, until a sufficient length has been covered.   To make a finish, the quill is turned back under the thread, the thread passed through the leather, pulled tight, and knotted (50–7423).

17.   The winding on Dakota pipe stems is a braid of four elements of which two are active and two passive.   The passive element consists of two strings laid parallel, over which are braided two quills crossing obliquely one over and one under (Fig. 30).   A similar technique has been described by Roth [1] (50–6336, 7858).

Fig. 30.   Technique No. 17.

18.   In this connection, we may mention a technique found on Lilard River.   The quills are passed over and under the strings of sinew which are

---

[1] Roth, 54.

in turn passed over and under similar sinew strings (Fig. 31). The whole, on being drawn tight together conceals the strings and presents a surface somewhat like fine beadwork[1] (50–3904, 3939).

As a summary, it appears that so far we have not found Nos. 3, 4 and 8 except among the Blackfoot. Of their other technique Nos. 1, 2 and 7 are used by the Gros Ventre, Nos. 1, 2 and 5 by the Assiniboine, Nos. 2 and 7 by the Sarcee and Nos. 6 and 7 by the Dakota. Among the Gros Ventre, we also find four types peculiar, among the Assiniboine, two and for the Dakota one. While this is in no sense complete, it indicates that considerable individuality may be expected for the different tribes, though these individualities tend to resolve themselves into minor variations of very

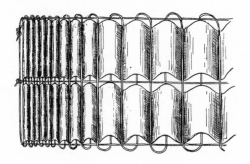

Fig. 31.   Technique No. 18.

widely distributed processes. The woven work, No. 18, is an interesting type and may well be the more primitive form of the intrusive woven beadwork highly developed among some woodland peoples.

Little could be learned as to native dyes used in quill work as for a long time the Blackfoot have used commercial dyes, the usual mode being to boil quills and feathers with pieces of print goods of the desired color. Maximilian observes:— "They [women] are likewise very skillful in the art of dyeing: and, to produce the beautiful yellow colour, they employ a lemon-coloured moss from the Rocky Mountains, which grows in the fir trees, my specimens of which are unfortunately lost. A certain root furnishes a beautiful red eye, and they extract many other bright colours from the goods procured from the Whites. With them they dye the porcupine quills and the quills of the feathers, with which they embroider very neatly."[2]

As yet, practically no woven beadwork is to be found among these people,

---

[1] See also Roth, 54.

[2] Maximilian, 103. McClintock, 276, identifies this moss as *Evernia vulpina*.

though it is rapidly spreading over the area. The usual form is to cover the surface of tanned skin with strung beads. The strands are sewed down at frequent but irregular intervals, giving a uniform beaded surface. This is in contrast to the prevailing Dakota, Crow, Cheyenne and Ute method of sewing all strands down at regular intervals, thus producing rows or ridges, exactly like quill work. On the other hand, the Northern Shoshone, Gros Ventre, and Assiniboine show tendencies to use the Blackfoot method, but not exclusively.

Feather Work. In attaching feathers the Blackfoot use several methods. We have observed two of the modes described by Dr. Kroeber as characteristic of the Arapaho and clearly shown in his Figs. 104a–b, and 105a.[1] Also in some cases the thong is passed through a slit in the quill. The more elaborate and varied techniques of the Arapaho are wanting. On the whole, the Blackfoot employ the feather much less than their immediate neighbors.

Skin Dressing. Among all the buffalo hunting tribes, the dressing of skins was an important household industry and in this respect the Blackfoot were no exception to the rule. It was not only woman's work, but her worth and virtue were estimated by her output. The art still survives, in spite of the fact that materials are limited to steer hides, occasional elk or deer skins and pelts of small animals used in ceremonial outfits; and that the commercial value of steer hides together with the cheapness of cloth tend to reduce the consumption of native tanned skins to a minimum. However, the continued use of the moccasin instead of the white man's shoe tends to preserve, at least, the cruder forms of the art. Soles of moccasins, parfleche and other similar bags are made of stiff rawhide, the product of one of the simplest and perhaps the most primitive methods of treating skins. The uppers of moccasins, soft bags, thongs, etc., are of pliable texture, produced by a more elaborate and laborious process. The skill to produce the latter is fast disappearing and such examples as came under our observation may be regarded as survivals from a past régime, from which supplemented by information in the field, the following partial reconstruction of an important industry has been made.

For the rawhide finish the treatment is as follows:— Shortly after the removal of a hide, it is stretched out on the ground near the tipi, hair side down and held in place by wooden stakes or pins, such as are used in staking down the covers of tipis. Clinging to the upturned flesh side of the hide are many fragments of muscular tissue, fat and strands of connective tissue, variously blackened by coagulated blood. The first treatment is that of cleaning or fleshing. Shortly after the staking out, the surface is gone over

---

[1] Kroeber, (b), 321.

with a fleshing tool by which the adhering flesh, etc., is raked and hacked away [1] (Plate I). This is an unpleasant and laborious process requiring more brute strength than skill. Should the hide become too dry and stiff to work well, the surface is treated with warm water. After fleshing, the hide is left to cure and bleach in the sun for some days, though it may be occasionally saturated by pouring warm water over its surface. The next thing is to work the skin down to an even thickness by scraping with an adze-like tool. The stakes are usually pulled up and the hard stiff hide laid down under a sun-shade or other shelter. Standing on the hide, the woman leans over and with a sidewise movement removes the surface in chips or shavings, the action of the tool resembling that of a hand plane (Plate III). After the flesh side has received this treatment, the hide is turned and the hair scraped away in the same manner. This completes the rawhide process and the subsequent treatment is determined by the use to be made of it.

The soft-tan finish as given to buffalo and deer hides for robes, soft bags, etc., is the same in its initial stages as the preceding. After fleshing and scraping, the rawhide is laid upon the ground and the surface rubbed over with an oily compound composed of brains and fat often mixed with liver.[2] This is usually rubbed on with the hands (Plate III). Any kind of fat may be used for this purpose though the preferred substance is as stated above. The writer observed several instances in which mixtures of packing house lard, baking flour, and warm water were rubbed over the rawhide as a substitute. The rawhide is placed in the sun, after the fatty compound has been thoroughly worked into the texture by rubbing with a smooth stone (Plate IV), that the heat may aid in its further distribution. When quite dry, the hide is saturated with warm water and for a time kept rolled up in a bundle. In this state, it usually shrinks and requires a great deal of stretching to get it back to its approximate former size. This is accomplished by pulling with the hands and feet, two persons being required to handle a large skin (Plate IV). After this, comes the rubbing and drying processes. The surface is vigorously rubbed with a rough edged stone until it presents a clean grained appearance (Plate V). The skin is further dried and whitened by sawing back and forth through a loop of twisted sinew or thong tied to the under side of an inclined lodge pole (Plate V). This friction develops considerable heat, thereby drying and softening the texture. As this and the preceding rubbing are parts of the same process their chrono-

---

[1] These pieces of flesh, fat, etc., are much prized for making soup. For an Assiniboine reference to the same practice, see Vol. 4, p. 136.

[2] McClintock states that the root of the parsnip, *Leptotaenia multifida*, was sometimes mixed with these, 274.

logical relation is not absolute, but the order, as observed, was usually as given above.[1] The skin is then ready for use.

Skins with the hair on, are treated in the same manner as above, except that the adze-tool is not applied to the hair side. A large buffalo robe was no light object and was handled with some difficulty, especially in the stretching.

No dressing of deer skins came under the observation of the writer, but a statement was secured from an old woman who still kept up the art. She proceeded as stated under soft tan, except that after the fatty compound had been worked into the skin, the hair surface was rubbed down with a beaming tool (now with a common knife, formerly with a rib bone) to remove any scattering hairs missed in working down with the adze. Then the skin was treated in the aforesaid manner and rubbed over a cord. The color and finish were imparted by smoking. The skins were spread over a frame similar to that of a sweat house, a hole was dug underneath and a smoulder-ing fire maintained with sage or rotten wood. My informant had a deer skin to which she had given the rawhide finish some time ago; later on, she expected to give it the soft tan and smoked finish.

A minute study of the above process for any of the northern Plains tribes will have doubtful comparative value because the influence of the fur trade upon the mode of dressing skins must have been strong and is certainly almost beyond discovery. Even as late as 1880, the Blackfoot traded hundreds of soft tanned buffalo robes at Fort Benton and elsewhere. During the trading period great stores of rawhide were accumulated during the hunting season to be tanned at leisure. Hence, the reader may expect a great deal of varia-tion in the process stated above and a great many modifications due to the demands of trade. However, a few comparative statements may not be out of place. The method of soft tan as described above, is practically the same as described by James.[2] While few writers are so explicit as this one, we get hints from many journals that indicate a general distribution of this process from Peace River to the Gulf of Mexico and from California to New England. Even the treatment of buckskin by smoking is known over this whole area, at least. However, the Kiowa processes as described by Battey are in greater agreement with those of the Blackfoot than all other accounts we have read.[3]

We may pass to a description of the instruments used by the Blackfoot. Unfortunately, the collection does not contain many specimens, but from

---

[1] See also James, 1, 202.

[2] James, 1, 202.

[3] Battey, 187.

observation and information procured in the field, the types can be shown. The adze-like scraper is the well known antler elbow type; Fig. 33c, is minus the metal blade but otherwise complete. The wrapping to the blade is held by a cord taking two turns around the handle and anchored in the end by a wire nail. In all tools of this type, the part of the handle forming the haft is usually wedge-shaped, flattened on the inner and rounded on the outer surface. The blade is placed on the flattened surface, wrapped to the haft by a strip of soft tanned skin and the whole wound by many turns of a small thong. In use, the downward pressure of the stroke wedges the blade tight by forcing the wedged haft down into the aforesaid binding. When the pressure is removed the blade and its binding may slip off unless held in place by the cord passing around the handle. Old people say that formerly, the blades were of chipped stone, but that iron has been in use for a very long time. The blades are now made of scraps of iron, often pieces of files, with slightly rounded ends on which are cutting edges bevelled from the outer surface. In operation, the blade is practically perpendicular to the surface to be scraped (Plate III).

Fleshers have iron blades, serrated, often the whole tool being made in the form of a common cold chisel. Until recently, fleshers had the form of a specimen collected among the Gros Ventre, Fig. 34d. In use, the shaft of the tool is grasped near the middle and the loop of thong above passed under the wrist as a brace (Plate I). No beaming tools were collected; but according to information they were of the rib bone type.

In 1906, the writer observed a woman removing the hair from a rawhide with a rounded waterworn pebble (Plate I). She struck hard glancing blows and at each stroke removed a small bunch of hair. In reality, the action was about the same as rubbing and notwithstanding the force of the impact the hide was not damaged, even the pigmented layer being practically intact. Further information was to the effect that this method was still used for various reasons, chiefly of convenience, and that in former times when making shields of buffalo hide the hair was removed in this way so as not to disturb the pigmented layer nor reduce the natural thickness of the hide. Many objects of buffalo hide in collections are covered with a chocolate-like layer, apparently the normal pigmented layer of the skin. Such a layer would be damaged by the use of the adze tool and the above may be a suggestion as to the manner of dressing so as to produce this effect.

At another time, a stone scraper was secured from an old woman about to dress a deer skin (Fig. 32). It is a slab struck from the outer surface of a waterworn pebble, the edge being formed by the fracture and the curved surface.[1] The owner claimed to have made many such implements but that

---

[1] Spinden refers to a similar stone scraper used by the Nez Perce, (b), 215.

suitable pebbles were found with great difficulty. In use, this tool was held and handled in the same manner as the unshaped pebble noted above. The owner stated that she preferred such a tool for work on a deer skin because metal tools cut too many holes. Before leaving this subject, it may not be amiss to note the distribution of the types of tools just described.

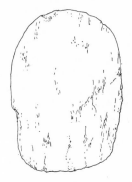

The adze tool as found in the collections of this Museum is used by the Sarcee, Blackfoot, Gros Ventre, Teton, Arapaho, Cheyenne, Comanche, Wind River and Lemhi Shoshone, and Turtle Mountain Ojibwa. According to Mason, the Crow, Kiowa, Pawnee, Paiute and a Pueblo group of New Mexico should be added; Long, the Omaha; De Smet, the Flatheads and Spinden, the Nez Perce. References to this instrument have not been found

Fig. 32 (50–6438). A Hide Scraper of Stone. Length, 11 cm.

in the literature for California and the coast northward, the Athapascan area nor the Eastern Woodlands, though the search was not exhaustive. The above indicates that it is peculiar to the Plains area and confined chiefly to the buffalo hunting tribes. The fact that a specimen occurs in the Ojibwa

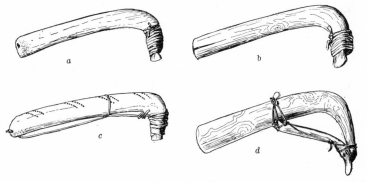

Fig. 33 *a* (50–6014), *b* (50–4760), *c* (50–2334), *d* (50–586a). Types of Scrapers. Length of *a*, 35 cm.

Collection from Turtle Mountain and not in other Ojibwa collections is in keeping with this statement. The adze tools in the Museum collections and those figured by Mason [1] are of four types as in Fig. 33. Their distribution with the number of specimens noted, is as follows:—

---

[1] Mason, (e), Plates CXII–CXIII.

a. Sarceė 2, Gros Ventre 1, Paiute 1, Wind River 1, Lemhi Shoshone 1, Teton 1, Nez Perce 1.

b. Comanche 2, Pueblo 1, Turtle Mountain Ojibwa 1.

c. Crow 1, Wind River Shoshone 3, Blackfoot 1.

d. Gros Ventre 1, Arapaho 3, Cheyenne 2.

The types *a* and *d* differ only in that *a* has handles of antler while *b* has a handle of wood. The distribution of these types as given above is, of course, tentative beyond the limits of the available material, but the table suggests a narrow range for the specialized types *b* and *c*.

The chisel-like fleshing tool with a rounded toothed edge is very widely distributed in North America east of California and the North Pacific Coast, seemingly characteristic of the forest areas. In the Museum collections and among the illustrated specimens described by Mason [1] appear the following types for the Plains area:—

a. Shaft from the tibia of buffalo, steer, etc., with joint and part of femur attached. (Fig. 34d.)

　i.   Bone edge; Isleta (New Mexico) 1, Teton 1.

　ii. Iron edge; small blade attached to shaft, Gros Ventre 2.

b. Shaft from the tibia alone, bone edge; Ute 3, Dakota 1. (Fig. 34b.)

c. Entire tool of iron; Teton 3, Sarcee 1, Arapaho 3, Cheyenne 1, Wind River Shoshone 1. (Fig. 34a.)

Mason [2] states that the iron flesher was used by the Kiowa; De Smet [3] by the Flathead. As shown by the Museum collection the shaft of this type is covered with rawhide. Mason [4] figures a flesher of bone like Fig. 34b and one with a wooden shaft and metal blade from the Indians of the Ungava district, while Turner [5] figures one of bone. Morice [6] remarks that the bone fleshers with serrated edges are known to the Carriers and the Tse'kehue but not to the Chilcotin, the former, in his opinion, having borrowed it from the Cree and other eastern Algonkins among whom it is common. This instrument is not mentioned by Teit [7] nor is it found in any of the collections from the plateaus and coast of British Columbia. Russell [8] collected one from the Dog Ribs. The writer has seen such tools from the Thaltan. On the other hand, he has not been able to learn of their use by the Iroquois. Thus, it seems that this tool has most likely been distributed

[1] Mason, (a), 275.
[2] Mason, (e), 571.
[3] De Smet, 1003.
[4] Mason, (e), Plate LXVIII.
[5] Turner, 293.
[6] Morice, (c), 70.
[7] Teit, 182.
[8] Russell, 177.

from the Algonkin area into the Mackenzie and Plains areas.   One also gets the impression from Mason that the flesher of the Plains is used as a graining tool by the forest tribes, but reference to Turner and Morice indicates that almost everywhere it is used primarily as a flesher.   About the only distinctive feature of Plains fleshers is the prevalence of the iron cold chisel type not observed outside of that area.   So far as the writer has observed, serrated bone fleshers of this type are not generally found in archaeological collections.   From the Mandan country, however, some are reported.[1]

Beaming tools are identified with the dressing of deer skins and in this

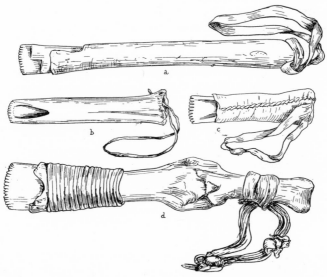

Fig. 34 *a* (50–3002) *b* (D–193), *c* (50–4382a), *d* (50–1770).   Types of Fleshers.   Length of *a*, 38 cm.

respect stand distinct from the adze tool used in dressing buffalo skins. They seem to be used wherever the dressing of deer skins is prevalent and best known under the following types:—

a.   Split leg bones.

b.   Combined tibia and fibula of deer or similar animal.

c.   Rib bone.

d.   Wooden stick with metal blade in middle, stick usually curved.

From the collection in this Museum it seems that the split leg bone type is not found in the Plains. Should further inquiry show this to be the case, it would be a matter of some interest since the split bone type is found in archaeological collections from British Columbia, Ohio and New York. The general aspect of the foregoing, is that the beaming tool is a concomitant of deer skin dressing from Point Barrow [1] and the Hupa,[2] to Labrador [3] and Pennsylvania.[4]

The rubbing of the skin over a twisted cord seems common to buffalo hunting tribes; for example, we find it among the Blackfoot, Gros Ventre, Arapaho, Dakota, Pawnee and Omaha from which its general distribution in the Plains may be inferred. The writer has not been able to find its mention outside of the Plains area. On the other hand, the rubbing with a rough stone is the usual treatment accorded deer skins. According to Maximilian,[5] the Indians of the upper Missouri used pumice stone. Long states that the Omaha used pumice stone, sharp stones or hoes and the same is said of the Pawnee.[6] The Museum collections contain a rounded piece from the porous end of a large bone said to have been used in skin dressing by the Cheyenne, possibly as a substitute for pumice stone. The collections from the Dakota and Arapaho contain flat rounded oval stones which are very smooth and oily. From the Dakota, the writer learned that such stones were used to rub in the fatty substance spread over the skin. One of these stones, from the Teton, has a rough fractured end and was used by the owner for the rough rubbing also.

A frame, or stage, for stretching hides was used by many tribes and is often met with among the Indians of the Plains. Though our information indicates the occasional use of such frames by the Blackfoot in the past, the almost invariable method of recent years is to stretch the skins upon the ground. The frame was used in winter when the ground was frozen too hard for driving stakes, but flat upon the surface and not horizontal.

Thus, in general, the implements used by the Blackfoot in dressing skins closely conform to the types of the buffalo hunting tribes which as a group show decided differences from those of other ethnographical areas. As among other tribes, women took pride in the number and quality of robes they dressed, often keeping records and referring to them when about to perform a ceremony.

Soft Bags and Pouches. Long slender bags for the smoking outfit were

---

[1] Mason, (e).
[2] Goddard.
[3] Turner.
[4] Heckewelder, 202.
[5] Maximilian, 125.
[6] James, 1, 203.

in use, Fig. 35 being the apparent type. They range in length from 70 to
100 cm. (fringe included) and in width from 10 to 17 cm. They taper
slightly toward the top and bear a fringe at the
bottom. The tips are usually cut so as to form
four ear-like flaps. A buckskin thong is fastened
to one side, the loose ends serving to tie the
mouth of the bag. The decoration is applied to
a small field at the base and to the edges of the
flaps at the mouth. The fringes are plain.

We collected one specimen much shorter and
wider than the typical pipe bags, fastened to one
side of which is a slender sheath for the pipe stem.
The decorations are also differently placed, suggesting foreign influence. However, the woman
from whom it was received claimed to have made
it. Another quill-worked bag lacks the flaps at
the top and bears the slats of rawhide wrapped
with quills, a characteristic of Dakota pipe bags.
This is an old piece concerning which no information as to the maker could be secured; the pre-
sumption is, that it is foreign.

In use, the tobacco, pipe bowl, stokers and
lighting implements are dropped into the bag,
while the stem, unless too short, protrudes from
the mouth, which is drawn tightly around it by
the closing thong. While the largest and most
highly ornamented bags are usually used by men,
women may use them without breach of propriety.
In general, however, those used by women are
smaller as are also their pipes. At present, the
most common form of pipe bag among both sexes
is a simple poke of cloth.

Fig. 35 (50–4424). A Pipe
Bag. Length 54 cm.

The only comparative data at hand is that of the collections in the
Museum. Pipe bags are especially conspicuous among the Dakota, where
they are much larger, ranging from 80 to 150 cm. in length, with proportion-
ate widths. At the end they have rows of rawhide strips wrapped with
quills. These do not hang free but are bound at the ends.[1] Below is a
fringe of buckskin. The decorated field is larger than in the Blackfoot
type and a narrow band extends up one border to the top, which is cut straight

[1] Wissler, (b).

and faced with beads or quills. A number of bags similar to the Dakota type were observed by the writer, among the Assiniboine of Fort Belknap reservation, and the collection made there contains a bag with a sheath for the stem similar in all respects to the one secured from the Blackfoot. The Cheyenne and the Crow seem to use pipe bags of the Dakota type. So far as the Museum collection goes, no pipe bags of either type appear among the Arapaho, Ute or Shoshone. They were rarely observed by the writer among the Gros Ventre. The Blackfoot type was found among the Lemhi Shoshone by Dr. Lowie.[1] Mr. Skinner also collected one of this type among the Cree near James Bay.

The ceremonial outfits of the Blackfoot contain tobacco pouches formed of animal and bird skins, reminding one of the medicine bags used by the central Algonkin. The skin of a very young antelope or deer was often used. This was removed entire by stripping back from the neck. Such bags are found in the collections from the Dakota, who claim this to have been the old, or parent form of pipe and tobacco bag. The fact that the general type of seamless bag is common and used for a variety of purposes may warrant a question as to whether the introduction of metal cutting and sewing implements during the historic period may not have influenced the development of these long, rectangular fringed pipe bags.

Fig. 36 (50–4428). A Paint Bag. Length, 26 cm.

Many of the paint bags used by the Blackfoot resemble their pipe bags (Fig. 36), even to the fringe and the flaps at the mouth. However, many paint bags in ceremonial outfits are without fringes or decorations of any kind. Some have square cut bases and some curved;[2] their lengths range from 8 to 15 cm. In some cases, those with square cut bases are provided with a pendant at each corner. Decorated paint bags of the fringed type

---

[1] Lowie, 212.

[2] Such curved bottom bags among the Dakota and elsewhere were formerly made from the scrotum of bull-calves and it is quite plausible that the form described above had its origin in this practice.

occur among the Gros. Ventre, Assiniboine, Arapaho, Sarcee, Dakota, and Shoshone. A specimen without the fringe appears in the Comanche collection. The Blackfoot, Sarcee, Gros Ventre, and Assiniboine use almost exclusively, bags with the flaps at the top, and bearing similar decorations. The Arapaho and Dakota incline to this type but also use those with straight tops. Among the Shoshone decorated paint bags are rare, but two specimens we have observed belong to these respective types. So far, it seems that the Arapaho alone, use the peculiar paint bag with a triangular tail, suggesting the ornamented pendants to the animal skin medicine bags of the Algonkin. However, we have seen a large bag of this pattern attributed to the Bannock.

A round-bottomed pouch with a decorated field and a transverse fringe was sometimes used for paint by the Blackfoot. The decorated part is on stiff rawhide while the upper is of soft leather, the sides and mouth of which are edged by two and three rows of beads respectively. This seems to be an unusual form for the Blackfoot and rare in other collections; while the related form frequently encountered in Dakota and Assiniboine collections has not been observed among the Blackfoot or their immediate neighbors.[1] The Blackfoot collection contains two small, flat rectangular cases with fringes. One of these was said to have been made for a mirror, the other for matches. However, such cases were formerly used by many tribes for carrying the ration ticket issued by the government. Their distribution seems to have been general in the Plains.

A type of pouch, usually said to have been used for strike-a-light, has not been found among the Blackfoot. It is usually made of stiff commercial leather and profusely beaded.[2] It is numerous among the Shoshone, Ute, Arapaho, Cheyenne, Dakota, Gros Ventre and the Assiniboine. Among the Arapaho and Gros Ventre we also find a very large pouch of the same pattern.[3]

Although the Blackfoot claim not to have used the peculiar large rectangular bags called by the Dakota "a bag for every possible thing," a type of which is illustrated in a former Museum publication,[4] one specimen of buffalo hide was secured from a Blood woman. It is similar in form and decoration to the bag just cited, except that it lacks a flap to close the mouth, as observed among some Gros Ventre specimens.[5] On the whole, the character of the quilled lines and the beaded designs on the ends, strongly sup-

[1] Wissler, (b), 236.
[2] Wissler, (b), Plate XLI.
[3] Kroeber, (b), 97.
[4] Wissler, (b), 243.
[5] Kroeber, (a), 164.

port the claim that this specimen was not made' by a Blackfoot woman. The current Indian name for such bags is Crow (Indian) bag. This type of bag occurs among the Assiniboine, the Gros Ventre, Dakota, Cheyenne, Arapaho, Ute, Shoshone and probably elsewhere with practically no variations either in form or decoration. Yet, the Bannock and the Nez Perce seem to make use of a small bag of this type, easily distinguished by a slight variation in decoration.

An interesting type of bag was made from the skins of antelopes' feet bearing the dew claws, two specimens of which occur in the collection. These were said to have been very common when game was abundant. Similar bags occur in the collections from the Ojibwa, northern Athapascan and eastern Cree. An Eskimo pouch made of birds' feet may be considered an analogous type [1] as well as some bags mentioned by Russell.[2] The Museum collection contains an interesting bag made of foot skins of the wild goose, joined by a beaded strip of skin, which is credited to the Mackenzie area. Mention may also be made of a Cheyenne paint bag made of the skin of a turtle's foot.

A unique undecorated bag made of buffalo hide deserves mention. This form was once in general use and had a special name, signifying "double bag" (Fig. 37). Although it has some resemblance to a saddle bag, it was said to have been used by women as a general carrying bag. So far, we have not encountered bags of this kind among other tribes, unless a specimen noted by Father Morice may be so classed.[3]

For gathering berries, the Blackfoot, like many other tribes, often used the whole skins of small animals. No specimens of decorated bladders were observed

Fig. 37.   A Carrying Bag.

as among the Gros Ventre, Arapaho and Dakota.[4] By barter, woven bags of the Sahaptin type are secured and used for various purposes.

Awl cases were of the type shown in Fig. 38. Unlike some other tribes, the women fastened these to the dress, either high up on the breast, or over the left shoulder so as to be easily reached with the hand. The awl cases

[1] Bulletin 15, 402.
[2] Russell, 175.
[3] Morice, (c), 148.
[4] Kroeber, (a), 167.

of the Dakota are of the same shape but have closing flaps. Curiously enough, those of the Blackfoot like those of the Assiniboine are almost always covered with blue beads.

From this brief comparative résumé, it appears that in the matter of soft decorated bags and pouches, the Blackfoot resemble most the Athapascan, Cree and other northern Algonkin tribes rather than their neighbors of the Plains. As in most other cases, a complete statement cannot be given until more data are available.

Formerly, young men carried small toilet bags of which Fig. 39 is said to be a type. The decorations on this bag suggest Cree influence but according to our information are of an unusual recent pattern. A similar bag is figured by Father Morice.[1] One noted by

Fig. 38 (50–5453).
A Bodkin Case.
Length, 23 cm.

Russell[2] was said to have been used for a strike-a-light outfit and for bullets. Dr. Lowie collected one of this type among the Assiniboine where it was regarded as a receptacle for war-medicine.[3]

Fig. 39 (50–4482).   A Toilet Bag for Young Men.
Length, 18 cm.

[1] Morice, (c), 148.
[2] Russell, 177.
[3] This series, Vol. 4, p. 32.

Beaded knife cases of the mere ornamental types found in the collections from the Dakota, Arapaho, Gros Ventre, Assiniboine, etc., are now rare among the Blackfoot. In fact, none but practical examples were encountered and these were rarely decorated. The same general condition holds for bodkin cases. The few beaded specimens observed, so closely agreed with those in use among several divisions of the Siouan stock as to render their foreign origin quite probable. As among the Assiniboine, the knife case for men was provided with an eye for the belt while that of the women was supported by a hanger.

Rawhide Bags. The collection contains a number of rectangular bags made from a single piece of rawhide cut as in Fig. 40. As to form, they are of two types — those opening on the longer side and those opening on the shorter side. All vary much in size, ranging from 20 to 60 cm., on the longest side. The proportions of the two sides on a denominator of 10, range from 6 to 9. They are closed by a flap as in Fig. 41 and are held in place by two thongs passed through as many holes in their edges. The edges are covered with cloth, either blue or red.

Fig. 40 (50–4578). A Bag ready for Sewing.

The sewing is by an over stitch, holes being punched in the edges of the rawhide through which a single thong is passed, always from the same side. Apparently this sewing starts from the bottom of the bag. A knot is tied in the thong, some distance from the end, so that in the finished bag, the loose ends hang freely from the corners, forming simple pendants. However, two bags in the collection are sewed with a single thread passing in and out instead of over the edge. The short carrying strap is fastened on the back near the top. One large bag is provided with a strap long enough to pass over the shoulders. The faces of these bags and the flaps are decorated with painted designs.

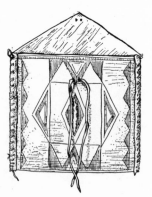

Fig. 41 (50–4459). A Bag. Length, 30 cm.

The Museum collections contain similar bags from the Sarcee, Gros

Ventre, Assiniboine, Cheyenne, Arapaho, Dakota, Shoshone, Bannock, Ute and Nez Perce. Practically all are of the same range in size and proportion as those used by the Blackfoot.[1] The over stitch and the cloth binding, red or blue, is almost uniform. A few Arapaho bags have the single thong in-and-out sewing. The pendants are equally universal. An additional pendant is found on a few Nez Perce and Gros Ventre bags produced by extending the cloth binding below the bottom. In general, it may be said that we have scarcely found a single structural detail peculiar to any one of the above-mentioned tribes. These bags are used by women rather than by men. The larger ones may contain skin-dressing tools, the smaller ones, sewing or other small implements, etc. Sometimes, they were used in gathering berries and other vegetable foods.

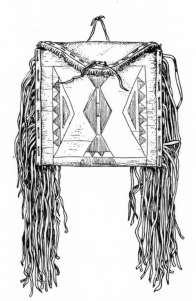

Fig. 42 (50–4448). A fringed Bag. Length, 35 cm.

For ceremonial purposes, the Blackfoot use a square bag of the above type with heavy side fringes, cut from a rectangular piece of hide with the strands still joined at one edge. This edge is inserted between the edges of the bag, and the whole sewed by a single thong passing in and out. In some cases, a strip of cloth is laid on the face edge of the bag. The edge of the flap may also be fringed and cloth bound, though this occurs but rarely (Fig. 42).

Among the Sarcee collections are bags in every way duplicating these. A single specimen from the Gros Ventre is also a duplicate and is probably of Blackfoot make. Two such duplicates appear in the Kootenai collection. From the Arapaho, we find one sewed with two thongs passing in and out from opposite sides. West of the mountains, another Blackfoot duplicate was collected among the Yakima, while another, said to have come from Oregon has the sewing observed in the Arapaho specimen. Some other

---

[1] Recently an unusual bag was collected among the Comanche. One specimen is 70 cm. wide by 39 cm. in depth, but otherwise its structure is of the type here noted.

bags of the same general shape among the Arapaho, Dakota and Nez Perce collections have a short fringe, formed by tying the ends of the thongs as described in Fig. 44. In passing, attention may be called to a bag of this type described by Teit [1] as common to the Thompson River Indians. However, since this specimen agrees in every detail with those just described, it is probable that it was brought in by trade.

A cylindrical rawhide case is used for many kinds of ceremonial objects

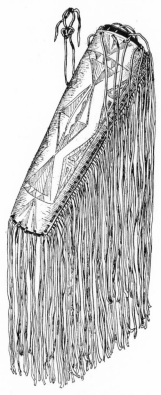

(Fig. 43). The usual type is formed by rolling up a piece of rawhide cut so as to form a tapering tube. The ends are closed by disks of the same material. These are fastened in a simple manner; a hole is punched in the margin of the disk and another in the margin of the tube; through these a long thong is passed and tied so that the free ends hang down at length. The cover can be lifted by opening the knots on one side and drawing the thongs partly out. The edges of the tube section are held in place by a single thong, passing in and out. However, the most distinctive feature in such cases is the fringe. This is formed as in rectangular bags, and held between the overlapping edges of the tube. The strands are longest at the top of the case, but the hanger is so placed that while the case itself takes a slanting position the ends of the strands are approximately horizontal. All the specimens of this type, observed by us, are of the same approximate size. The length of the case in six specimens measured, ranges from 50 to 58 cm. The fringes vary in extreme lengths from 40 to 80 cm. So far as examined, all are made exactly like Fig. 43.

Fig. 43 (50–4511). A Medicine Case. Length, 60 cm.

In the collection there are a number of small cases of similar structure. These range from 31 to 36 cm. in length (Fig. 44). Curiously enough, they are like the larger ones, except in the manner of joining the edges of the tube; pairs of holes are made at regular intervals through which thongs are tied, the ends forming a scattering fringe. The edge may be faced with cloth as

---

[1] Teit, 203.

on some rectangular bags. When so faced, the edges overlap, otherwise they do not.

The collections contain one unusual specimen about 50 cm. long, without a cover but otherwise structurally somewhat like the small cases. Its decoration, however, is different from that of both the large and small types just described. In the Museum collections are some large Sarcee and Gros Ventre cases of the Blackfoot type except that the fringes are tied in as with the small Blackfoot cases. The Nez Perce cases have very long fringes formed by separate or double thongs, giving the general appearance of those of the Blackfoot. The Arapaho cases are seldom fringed at the side and the bottoms are close fitting, secured by a two thong in-and-out stitch. The sides are joined by a similar stitch. The Dakota cases have very short fringes formed by tying the thongs, as in small Blackfoot specimens, while the bottoms are heavily fringed. The Assiniboine seem more like the Dakota than otherwise. Shoshone cases vary a great deal in fringes and shapes, though all examined have the over edge stitch for the sides. The most peculiar form is that of the Ute, the covers and bottoms are somewhat larger in diameter than the case; the fringe is at the bottom and hangs over the projecting edge of the disk. The Comanche collection contains a case peculiar in that it tapers from the bottom to the top, or the reverse of the usual form. It has the fringe at the bottom like the Ute, but lacks the projecting edge of the disk.

Fig. 44 (50–4473). A small Medicine Case. Length, 31 cm.

Parfleche. Perhaps one of the most characteristic rawhide objects in the whole area is the parfleche. Its simplicity of construction is inspiring and its usefulness scarcely to be over-estimated. Among the Blackfoot, they are always decorated in a characteristic manner. To make a parfleche, the Blackfoot women begin on a cow-hide, formerly that of a buffalo, that has been pegged out on the ground hair side down. After the fleshing, the surface is laid out for as many parfleche as it will make; the remainder of the space is given over to bags or reserved for moccasin soles. The painting is done at this time. Fig. 45 shows the outline of a steer hide with design for 2 parfleche and 2 bags.[1] Finally, when this side is finished, the skin is taken up, thrown upon the ground, hair side up and scraped as described under a previous heading. Then the woman marks out with the point of a

---

[1] In addition the designs for three toy parfleche have been laid out on the hide. A bag cut out and ready for sewing is shown in Fig. 40.

Fig. 45 (50–4565).   A painted Hide for Parfleche and Bags.   Length, 160 cm.

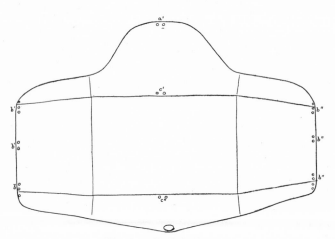

Fig. 46.   A Parfleche Pattern.

knife, the outline of the parfleche, bags etc., after which they are cut out. With a little trimming, they are ready for folding. The approximate form for a parfleche is shown in Fig. 46, and its completed form in Fig. 47. The side outlines as in Fig. 46 are irregular and show great variations, none of which can be taken as certainly characteristic. To fill the parfleche, it is opened out as in Fig. 46, and the contents arranged in the middle. The large flap is then brought over and held by lacing a′, a″. The ends are then turned over and laced b′, b″. The closed parfleche may then be secured by both or either of the looped thongs at c′, c″.

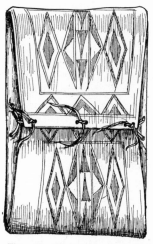

Fig. 47 (50–4422). A Parfleche. Length, 56 cm.

Primarily, the parfleche was used for holding pemmican, though dried meat, dried berries, tallow, etc., found their way into it when convenient. In recent years, they seem to have more of a decorative than a practical value; or rather, according to our impression, they are cherished as mementos of buffalo days, the great good old time of Indian memory, always appropriate and acceptable as gifts. The usual fate of a gift parfleche is to be cut into moccasin soles.

While there is great uniformity in the parfleche of the Missouri-Saskatchewan area, some interesting differences may be noted. The range in size as found in the Museum collections, may be seen from the following average measurements:—

	Length.	Width.
Blackfoot	60	38
Sarcee	61	38
Gros Ventre	67	31
Nez Perce	66	32
Crow	68	36
Kootenai	62	38
Arapaho	63, 75	40
Dakota	63	37
Assiniboine	63	36
Shoshone	80	38
Ute	81	38
Bannock	78	35

From our measurements, it appears that there are two length types, the longer of which prevails among the Shoshone, Ute and Bannock. The shorter seems to prevail among the Siouan and Algonkin groups and in particular, in the areas contiguous to the Blackfoot habitat. The Arapaho collections seem to contain representatives of both types. While this collection is by far the largest in the Museum, the diversity in size cannot be attributed to this alone, since from the Nez Perce we have an almost equal number whose sizes are quite uniform. Curiously enough, the widths are not correlated to the lengths, but remain fairly constant. Blackfoot parfleche have tapering flaps. This cannot be considered accidental, because when the design is painted as just described, its sides are made to slant in the same manner. The same feature is observable for the Assiniboine, Sarcee, Kootenai and a Comanche specimen. The other tribes fold their parfleche straight. The lacing in the ends of the flaps, varies in that the Crow, Arapaho, Gros Ventre, Ute, Shoshone and Nez Perce use a single lace in the middle with one pair of holes. The Assiniboine, Kootenai and Sarcee use the same method as the Blackfoot. The Dakota also use a single pair of holes but often place a single hole at each corner as well.

In general, it may be said that the Blackfoot type of parfleche is characterized by the angling flaps, the three pairs of lace holes and the side loops. The latter seems peculiar to them; the former are shared by the Assiniboine, Sarcee, Kootenai and perhaps by the Comanche.

Pipes. These are used by both men and women; those of the women, however, being much smaller than those carried by men. The pipe in Fig. 48 may be taken as the typical man's pipe. The bowl is of dark stone inlaid at the base with a band of lead. The stem is decorated with three

Fig. 48 (50–5437).   A Man's Pipe.   Length, 64 cm.

sections of wound brass wire. A woman's pipe of slightly different form is shown in Fig. 49. The stem has three windings of horse hair similar to those of wire, in the preceding. In this case, the stem has been split and the two halves grooved to form the bore, after which they were bound together by the hair wrappings.

Pipe stokers are usually short pointed sticks, in contrast to the long ones used by the Dakota, Arapaho, and some other tribes. Sometimes a ball of charcoal is placed in the bottom of the bowl before filling with tobacco, to prevent the contents of the pipe from working up into the stem. The stems are almost without exception round, rather heavy and worked down to a smooth surface. The wood is of ash or other hard wood, selected in the natural round of the proper size and length from which the bark and sap layer are scraped before polishing. The holes in the stems are burned out with rods of iron. How they were made before the introduction of iron

Fig. 49 (50–8). A Woman's Pipe. Length, 19 cm.

by white traders is not known, but is suggested by the split stem to the woman's pipe, Fig. 49.

The bowls were made of a dark greenish stone found in many parts of the Blackfoot habitat. When first removed from the strata, this stone is easily worked down with a file. In course of time, the stone becomes hard and the heat from smoking turns the bowl a dull black. Some old people stated that according to tradition, stone pipe bowls were not made before the introduction of iron tools. Blocks of hard tough clay were cut into the form of a pipe bowl, rubbed with grease and hardened over the fire and by use. This is in agreement with the traditions concerning pottery but seems unlikely. Pipe bowls of red catlinite are often seen but these are of different shapes and are brought in by gift or barter. Fine pipes of

Fig. 50 (50–4872). An Inlaid Pipe secured in Trade. Length, 11 cm.

black stone, inlaid with catlinite and other materials are also brought in from the Flathead country (Fig. 50).

Tools. Information concerning a few tools came to hand, chiefly those surviving the régime of the trader. Sticks and arrow shafts were smoothed and worked down by two grooved stones of the well known type. However, they were oval rather than elongated rectangular. Shafts were straightened by a kind of wrench made by boring a hole in a piece of "boss rib." A peculiar kind of spoke-shave was made of a stone flake set in a curved cut in the middle of a stick. We observed an old man working down a piece of wood for a cane with an unmounted flake (Plate II). Little saws made of scrap iron were used to cut the notches in arrow shafts, for inserting the points. Holes in objects were usually made by burning, but small ones were drilled with arrows, the shaft being twisted between the hands. There was knowledge of neither pump nor bow drills.

In former times, wood for the fire was broken with the knees and hands or with stone headed mauls. Henry writes of the Piegan in 1811 that, "Many families are still destitute of either a kettle or an ax. The women, who are mere slaves, have much difficulty in collecting firewood. Those who have no axes fasten together the ends of two long poles, which two women then hook over dry limbs of large trees, and thus break them off. They also use lines for the same purpose; a woman throws a line seven or eight fathoms long over a dry limb, and jerks it until the limb breaks off. Others again set fire to the roots of large trees, which having burned down, the branches supply a good stock of fuel. The trunk is seldom attacked by those who have axes, as chopping blisters their hands. Axes broken in

Fig. 51 (50–11). A Knife Sharpener. Length, 6 cm.

two pieces are still used by putting the fractured ends together and stretching over them the green gut of a buffalo, which, when dry, binds the pieces tightly. As such repairing soon wears loose, a fresh gut is put on."

According to Grinnell, grooves in arrows were produced by pushing the shafts through a hole in a flat bone, the circumference of the hole being provided with a small projecting spun.[2]

An object in the collection formed of two bears teeth bound together by colored horse's hair is said to be a knife sharpener (Fig. 51).

Musical Instruments. This aspect of culture is not well represented. The most common instrument is the hand drum. In recent years, at least, it is made by stretching cow skin over a broad hoop of wood. One side is open. The cover is secured by nails and cross cords of twisted thong placed at right angles. The crossing of these cords is wrapped with cloth to form the grip (Fig. 52). The beater is a short, slightly curved stick wrapped with cloth. When properly stretched, these drums give out a deep mellow tone. Large drums are now used at the sun dance and other general dances. If not the regular bass drum of white manufacture, they are of similar construction, formed by stretching skin over the ends of a wooden wash tub.

---

[1] Henry and Thompson, 724.
[2] Grinnell, (a), 200.

No doubt, in former years, large drums were made in the same manner; i. e., by stretching skin over a hollowed section of a tree. A fine example of this is to be seen in the Museum's Shoshone collection.[1]

Rattles varied in size and form according to the ceremonies in which they were used. The most common type is that shown in Fig. 53. The bulb is shaped from wet skins by a sand filling. When dry, the sand is shaken out and a wooden handle inserted.[2] The handle is well wrapped with thong and its connection with the bulb often concealed by a cover of

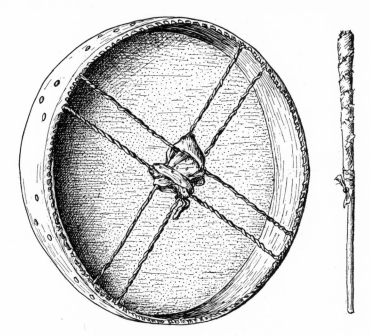

Fig. 52 (50–6892 a, b).   A Drum.   Diameter, 40 cm.

cow skin. A ring-shaped rattle is used by some societies. So far as could be learned, the flat disk rattle of the Central Algonkins was never used. Selected pebbles are used for the rattling, the most prized of which are secured in trade with Flathead Indians.

The simple whistle of bone, usually from the wing of an eagle, is found in most ceremonial outfits. The vent is plugged with resin and sometimes further adjusted by wrappings of sinew (Fig. 54). Many are so made

[1] This series, Vol. 2, 207.
[2] See also Henry and Thompson, 731.

as to be blown from either end, giving a different note in each case. All such whistles are usually provided with a hanging strap for the neck.

The flageolette was known and used to some extent; but according to

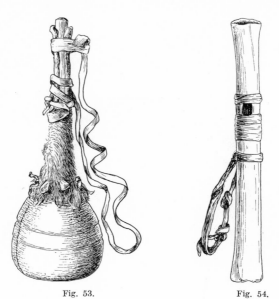

Fig. 53.   Fig. 54.

Fig. 53 (50–4462). A Rattle. Length, 28 cm.
Fig. 54 (50–5432). A Whistle. Length, 14 cm.

our judgment, to a much less degree than among the Dakota. We have seen but one specimen. This was of the four hole type. Curiously enough, it was made from part of a gun barrel, a form said to be used by the Cree.

TRANSPORTATION.

According to tradition, the prehistoric Blackfoot travelled on foot, assisted by dogs in the transportation of their effects. The horse seems to have been introduced before the tribe came into positive historical notice, the evidence for which will be presented at another time. At present, it may suffice to state that it must have been earlier than 1776. If canoes were ever used, the fact has long been lost to tradition. This would naturally follow from a long occupation of their historic habitat where the streams are too shallow for practical navigation. They seem never to have used the bull-boat of the several tribes on the Upper Missouri [1] but often used an analogous form of improvised raft. When a deep stream was to be passed with camp equipage, the skin covers of the tipis were folded into large dish-shaped bundles supported by cross pieces of wood, forming a kind of raft, upon which children, old people and baggage were placed and ferried across. These rafts were towed by the able-bodied men and women, usually the latter, swimming out and holding the lines with their teeth. The reports of the Palliser Expedition mention the services of the Blackfoot in ferrying baggage in circular boats, formed by wrapping the packages in leather tents. [2] From our own information it appears that the tow lines were sometimes attached to swimming horses. War parties made crude rafts of brush or logs upon which they placed such equipages as would be damaged by water, the men themselves, unless ill or wounded, swimming with a tow line held by the teeth. [3]

As since horse days, there was little travel on foot, packing is scarcely a feature. Its only form is found in the carrying of firewood by the women. The bundles of brush wood are held by a line, but not the familiar form with a head band, though this seems to have been used at times. The wood is usually made up into a bundle and secured by the line; then swung to the shoulders and held in place by the ends of the line in the hands. [4]

Cradles. The baby transports or cradles, we have seen were made over a board or frame not unlike those of some Shoshonean tribes. Fig. 55 shows the form very well. A kind of fur-lined pocket with sides braced with rawhide is attached for holding the infant. The large curved head of the board

---

[1] Kroeber credits the Gros Ventre with the bull-boat, but this may refer to the Blackfoot makeshift instead: though seemingly confirmed by Maximilian, 233.

[2] Further Papers relative to the Exploration of British North America, 1859, 9.

[3] For an incident mentioning the use of such a raft see myth, this series, Vol. 2, 77.

[4] For interesting touches of life in the use of this line see myths, Vol. 2, 58, 110.

is decorated with quill and beaded designs.   The form of these cradles is precisely that of the Nez Perce[1] as noted by Mason.   In the same article, a Blackfoot cradle of the Siouan type is shown, but this may belong to a division of the Dakota having the same name.

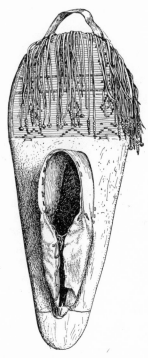

Fig. 55 (50–6164).   A Baby Board.
Length, 92 cm.

The Travois.   When dogs were used for transportation, they were usually harnessed to a kind of drag frame, the familiar travois.[2]   This was probably in use long before the introduction of horses, though there is little direct evidence on this point.   A similar travois of larger dimensions was used with horses, and notwithstanding the fact that wagons were issued to the Blackfoot more than thirty years ago, the horse travois is still in general use among the older women.   On the other hand, dog travois have not been in use for many years. According to our information, there were two types of travois.   One of these is shown in Fig. 56.   The sides of the frame are two poles locked together at the top with many turns of sinew and bent so as to converge like the arms of a Y.   About midway, these arms are crossed by a netted oval formed by bending a stick into the desired shape and weaving across with thongs.   The warp is stretched lengthwise of the oval hoop and the weft introduced by wrapping as figured by Mason.[3]   The ends of the oval are lashed to the poles by a thong which is spirally carried upward on one pole almost to the crotch of the Y, where it crosses over and is brought down the other pole in the same manner, in order to lash the corresponding end of the oval.   The crotch is wrapped about with a piece of skin dressed in the hair, forming a pad, or

---

[1] Mason, (b), 187.

[2] For probable origin of the term, note the following:— "*Travail à cheval,* pl. *travails à cheval,* literally horse-litter, also called in English *travail, travaille, travois, traverse,* and *travee.* The French plural is often erroneously given as *travaux,* as if it were the plural of *travail,* meaning "work"; but it has nothing to do with this, the etymology of the word being from Lat. *trabeculum,* diminutive of *trabs,* a beam, through such forms as *travallum* and *trabale,* meaning a trave, brake, or shackle."   (Henry and Thompson, 142).

[3] Mason, (c), 231.

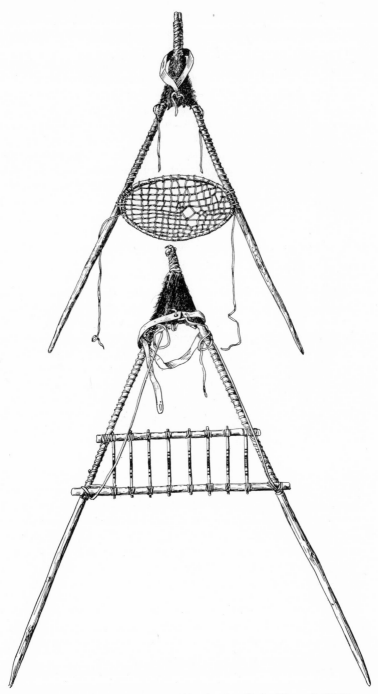

Fig. 56 a (50–5724, b (6158). Types of Travois. Length of a, 225 cm.; b, 307 cm.

saddle, for the shoulders of the dog. Soft pliable thongs are fastened to the ends of the oval by which the pack or load can be held in place. A broad band of rawhide which when in use passes around the dog's neck is fastened to the top of the saddle and carried over the legs of the Y. Two narrow thongs, one fastened to each pole just back of the saddle, serve as a cinch.

Another specimen in the collection also designed for a dog, differs from the preceding in that instead of the netted oval, there is a long rectangular frame with eight transverse bars lashed with sinew at intervals of about 10 cm., giving the whole the appearance of a ladder. The same curious mode of lashing the carrying frame is found in this specimen; the thong, however, is first tied to the saddle then carried loosely down to the lower cross bar of the frame where the lashing begins. It is then carried spirally up the pole to the second cross bar which is lashed in turn; then the thong is carried up the pole as before, crossing under the saddle and then passing spirally down the other pole, lashing the other ends to the bars, after which the lower end is brought up and fastened to the saddle as at the start. These lower ends are used in making up and securing the pack. Another difference between this and the preceding travois is in the length of the poles, 2.2 meters in the preceding case and 3 meters in this. According to our informants, the latter was about the usual length, though it naturally varied with the size of the dog. In this connection, the statement of Henry [1] that travois poles were long and were sometimes made of lodge-poles is of interest as a check upon our informants. Also, Catlin speaks of the Sioux dog travois as having poles about fifteen feet long.[2]

The horse travois, though much larger, is identical in structure with the type just described except that there is no saddle and that the poles cross at the apex with long slender extended ends (Plate VIII). The projection of these ends out above the horse's head is probably a conventionality. In use, the travois is usually fastened to a saddle upon which the woman rides. The part of the lashing thong that crosses from one pole to the other usually passes over the horn or projecting parts of the saddle while the poles are tied down at the sides or held in place by the weight of the rider. The purpose of the peculiar lashing noticed in all travois is now apparent; the draft is by the thong and not by the poles. In the dog travois where the crossing thong is concealed in the saddle, the breast strap, or yoke, is fastened by a thong passing through the saddle and around the crossing thong. By this ingenious contrivance, the pull is upon the pack frame rather than upon the poles and the possibility of the load being lost by the poles pulling out is reduced to a minimum.

---

[1] Henry and Thompson, 142.
[2] Catlin, 1, 45.

An interesting point in this connection is the general belief among the Blackfoot that the net type was generally used with dogs and the ladder type with horses. It will be observed that the apex of the dog travois differs in construction from that of the horse travois, the latter being formed by a mere crossing of the poles with long diverging ends, while in the former, the poles are bent to a parallel position and securely lashed with sinew.

Horse travois are still used for hauling wood and other camp supplies. In former times, the aged, the sick, and children were placed upon skins upon the frame of the travois, protected from the sun and rain by a canopy of the same material.[1] Some of the old people state that they saw children and even aged persons transported on dog travois; that the dogs were large and stronger than now, some of them standing about seventy-five cm. in height; that many dogs were able to drag tipi poles and that the strongest ones hauled skin tipi covers. That these statements are near the truth appear from the estimates of a dog's carrying capacity by white observers; thus Gass, speaking of the Tetons, says the dogs will haul about seventy pounds each.[2] The arrangement of the load on the frame is such that the dog bears considerably less than the total weight on his shoulders and as the friction of the ends of the drag-poles upon the ground cannot have been great, these estimates do not seem unreasonable.

It appears that formerly, before horses became numerous, some selective breeding was practised to provide large, strong dogs for travois use; but no detailed information could be secured. Within the memory of persons now living, male dogs were sometimes castrated "to keep them at home and make them quiet." In performing the operation, the dog was hitched to the travois and one hind leg bound firmly to one of the poles. That this was an aboriginal custom is doubtful. In recent times, horses were castrated by medicine men with the object of increasing their practical value, but no evidence was found that the idea of selective breeding was associated with the custom.[3]

The distribution of the travois cannot be stated definitely, but seems to have been general in the Missouri-Saskatchewan area. Specimens of the netted hoop type from the Dakota and Assiniboine[4] are found in the Museum's collections; those of the former for horses, the latter for dogs. Henry observed this type among the Assiniboine when dogs were used and implies that the same was used for horses.[5] Franklin saw the same type for dogs

---

[1] See Densmore for an illustration.

[2] Lewis and Clark, 1, 140.

[3] We found no confirmation of Maximilian's statement that buffalo were castrated by Indians; 290.

[4] According to McDougall, 69, the Stoney Assiniboine did not use the travois.

[5] Henry and Thompson, 518.

used by the Cree.[1]   Dr. William Jones collected a model of this type among the Ojibway in Minnesota.   The rectangular frame type has been reported among the Plains Cree,[2] Gros Ventre, Sarcee[3] and Arapaho.[4]

On the other hand, the Crow seem not to have used the travois at all. So far as the data at hand go, the Blackfoot dog travois are the only ones in which the poles do not cross at the apex;[5] in all other cases, whether for dogs or horses, the poles cross and project as in the Blackfoot horse travois. Among several southern tribes, the travois appears to have no fixed form but seems to be an improvised affair of tipi poles and packs, as among the Pawnee,[6] Kiowa[7] and Comanche.[8]   In some cases, the pack is placed upon the back of the horse while the poles drag behind; in others, two or more cross pieces are adjusted to the poles upon which the packs are placed as observed by Grinnell among the Pawnee.   Catlin speaking of a moving Sioux camp, indicated that the dogs were harnessed to a real travois while the horses dragged the improvised affairs of tipi poles and packs.[9]   Thus, we find the same peculiar variation from the crude to the definite as noted in the case of the bull-boat and the raft made of tipi covers.   So far as the information at hand goes, the real travois was prevalent among the tribes north of the Platte; the Blackfoot using both of the prevailing types, one for dogs and one for horses.   Statements by Morice and Spinden make it probable that formerly, all dog transportation on the interior plateau among the Athapascan, Salish, etc., was by packing, the travois being unknown.   Thus, the Crow seem to resemble the plateau tribes rather than those of the Plains.

Riding Gear.   Saddles of their own manufacture were formerly in use among the Blackfoot.   These seem to have been of three types.   As a rule, women used a saddle with a very high pommel and cantle similar to those used by the women of many other Plains Indians.   Yet all the specimens we saw in the field were similar to Fig. 57.   Men, however, used a pad saddle or a frame saddle with tree and cantle of elk horn and side bars of wood.   Two of these types are accurately described by Henry:—

"The saddles these people use are of two kinds.   The one which I suppose to be of the most ancient construction is made of wood well joined, and covered with raw

---

[1] Franklin, 100.

[2] Hector and Vaux, 250; and Blackfoot informants.

[3] Hill-Tout, 61.

[4] Kroeber, (b), 24.

[5] Since this was written a dog travois was collected among the Hidatsa by G. L. Wilson, in which the poles do not project and are joined somewhat like those in Fig. 56.   The poles are also of the same length in each.

[6] Grinnell, (b), 279.

[7] Whippel, 21.

[8] Catlin, 2, Fig. 166.

[9] Catlin, 1, 45, Fig. 21.

buffalo hide, which in drying binds every part tight. This frame rises about ten inches before and behind; the tops are bent over horizontally and spread out, forming a flat piece about six inches in diameter. The stirrup, attached to the frame by a leather thong, is a piece of bent wood, over which is stretched raw buffalo hide, making it firm and strong. When an Indian is going to mount he throws his buffalo robe over the saddle, and rides on it. The other saddle, which is the same as that of the Assiniboine and Crees, is made by shaping two pieces of parchment on dressed leather, about 20 inches long and 14 broad, through the length of which are sewed two parallel lines three inches apart, on each side of which the saddle is well stuffed with moose or red deer hair. Under each kind of saddle are placed two or three folds of soft dressed buffalo skin, to keep the horse from getting a sore back." [1]

No pack saddles were made. The stirrups were usually covered with skin from the scrotum of a buffalo bull. The types of saddle just described are found in collections from the Shoshone, Dakota, Gros Ventre, Cheyenne, Comanche and Crow and were doubtless in general use wherever the horse was common. Franchère notes a similar difference between men and women's saddles among the Sahaptin and Salish, the former using the pad-saddle, the latter, the frame with high pommel like those used by "Mexican ladies." [2] This is also affirmed by the Shoshone. [3] The Hidatsa also had both types. According to our personal information, saddles of the high-pommel type were rarely used by men in any part of the

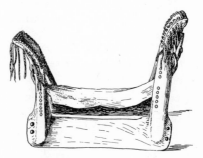

Fig. 57 (50–7433). A Saddle. Length, 34 cm.

Missouri-Saskatchewan area, though pad-saddles and those of the low pommelled frame type were often used by women as well as men. [4] As a matter of interest, the following characteristics of the woman's saddle may be noted:— The side bars are of wood, varying in length from 35 to 50 cm.; about 8 cm. in width and approximately one half a centimeter in thickness. These measurements are rather uniform in the various specimens examined. The pommels vary in height from 31 to 40 cm. The greatest difference appears to be in the breadth, or distance between the lower edges of the side bars, 19–29 cm. Unlike the saddles used by whites, the bow and cantle are of the same general form. The former, however, is often slightly higher and

---

[1] Henry and Thompson, 526; see also Maximilian, 251; Harmon, 291.

[2] Early Western Travels, 6, 341.

[3] Lewis and Clark, 3, 31.

[4] McDougall, 131, in speaking of a trip to Fort Garry in 1864 says, "we had two Indian pads as the Mexican saddle had not yet made its appearance so far north."

more nearly perpendicular. In fact, the fork, or bow, often leans inward, while that of the rear, or cantle, leans outward. The forward horn is provided with a hook and the rear with an eye in the corresponding position. Between them is suspended a piece of rawhide upon which the weight of the rider is supposed to rest.[1] The hook has apparently become conventional, because it is found on saddles where this support is not used and the eye is wanting, though these are said to be degenerate forms. The bows are bound to the side bars by thongs and the whole covered with rawhide as just stated.

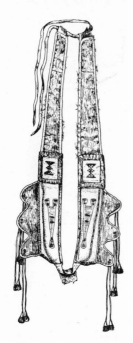

The frame saddles used by men and sometimes by women have their side bars joined by bows of elk horn. Sometimes y-shaped pieces of the same material are used but never with high pommels. The method of cinching is the same throughout, a strip of hide, fastened to the ends of the side bar where two holes are bored, to the middle of which the cinch is fastened. The pad-saddle is cinched by a flap on each side in much the same way.

Women's saddles are provided with cruppers of a peculiar shape (Fig. 58). The two wide rectangular portions are usually decorated by beadwork and fringes, while just above this is a small square of distinct ornamentation. This peculiar arrangement of decorated fields is found in Blackfoot, Gros Ventre, Cheyenne and Shoshone cruppers in the Museum's collections. The Sarcee cruppers, however, have rounded fields of decoration instead.

Fig. 58   (50–4500).   A
Crupper.

No decorated, specially designed saddle blankets, such as are used by the Shoshone and Dakota, were seen by the writer among the Blackfoot; however, he failed to seek information on this point. Maximilian mentions the use of a "large panther's skin for a housing."

Saddle bags of the type shown in Fig. 59 were in general use. In several specimens measured, the bag proper ranged from 123 to 131 cm. in length and 40 to 49 cm. in width, with fringes at the ends of from 29 to 48 cm. The outer surface of the bag bears two decorated fields from 29 to 38 cm. in length. The under surface is plain with a transverse slit, or mouth, in the

---

[1] For a slight variant of this type with a double side bar see Early Western Travels, 5, 144.

middle. Similar bags have been collected among the Dakota and Cheyenne, but so far as our observation goes, are neither so long nor so wide as those of the Blackfoot. Also, they have a transverse slit, or mouth, to one side and through both sides of the bag. Some specimens secured among the Sarcee are practically identical with those of the Blackfoot. Bags of this type are mentioned by Larpenteur, as common in the Missouri Area, who implies that the shape is copied after those used by whites.[1] Morice credits the Carriers with similar bags used on dogs.[2]

Formerly, the only bridle used for horses was a long rope, consisting of a single strand of buffalo skin, or several strands of the same material plaited. Braided hair ropes were also used. There is one in the Museum collection which is said to be made of human hair, members of a family sometimes saving their own hair for that purpose. This specimen was said to contain, in addition, hair from scalps taken in war. Maximilian mentions ropes made of buffalo hair, but we have no information on this point.[3] The Museum specimen is 8.7 m. long and for the greater part of its length seems to be four-ply. A red cord has been carried back and forth through the braid, apparently for ornament. There are two other ropes in the collection, one a simple strand of skin about 1 cm. in width

Fig. 59 (50–4407). A Saddle Bag. Length 130 cm.

and the other, a four-ply braid of similar material; their lengths are 5.9 and 9.4 m. respectively. The braided rope is provided with an eye of rawhide for the noose, while the others have iron rings. Thus it seems that three kinds of ropes were in use.

---

[1] Larpenteur, 67–8.
[2] Morice, (c), 148.
[3] Maximilian, 251.

In use, the rope was looped around the lower jaw. When running buffalo or when on the war path, the rider tucked the long end of the rope under the belt, so that if thrown, he would have some chance of catching it as it payed out or trailed along the ground. An ingenious bridle was often devised by opening the noose to the approximate extent of a bridle rein and passing it around the lower jaw in a double half-hitch. When dismounting, the rider holds on by the long end of the rope, which, when pulled forward, closes the noose down upon the animal's neck thus holding him halter fashion.

According to Lewis, the Shoshone used ropes of buffalo hair, plaited of six or seven strands of rawhide. In use, "it is first attached at one end about the neck of the horse with a knot that will not slip, it is then brought down to his under jaw and being passed through the mouth imbraces the under jaw and tongue in a simple noose formed by crossing the rope underneath the jaw of the horse. This when mounted he draws up on the near side of the horse's neck and holds in the left hand, suffering it to trail at a great distance behind him — sometimes the halter is attached so far from the end that while the shorter end serves him to govern his horse, the other trails on the ground as before mentioned." [1] This differs somewhat from the Blackfoot method just described, but was probably known to them also. Horse hair ropes are mentioned by Franchère [2] as common, west of the Mountains and rawhide thongs among the Pawnee by Grinnell. [3] The Museum collection contains braided ropes and simple thongs from the Dakota, Cheyenne and Shoshone. All of the braided ropes we have examined are four-ply.

Quirts were in general use among the Blackfoot. Those in the collection have handles of wood with double lashes of thong. These handles, are approximately 35 cm. in length, indicating some fixed standard of size, while the lashes vary from 55 to 65 cm. For about 12 cm. of their length, the latter are wrapped with red cloth or thongs. Though sometimes carved, the handles are usually plain. Formerly, handles of elk horn were common. Men sometimes used quirts with heavy club-like handles. All quirts were provided with wrist guards, often elaborately ornamented.

Taken as a whole, the horse trappings of the Blackfoot are not distinctive but of the types generally diffused among all the horse-using tribes. [4] It is reasonable to assume that these objects were introduced with the horse and so gradually worked their way northward and westward.

As with riding gear and trappings, the domestication and care of the

---

[1] Lewis and Clark, 3, 31.
[2] Early Western Travels, 6, 340.
[3] Grinnell, (b), 279.
[4] Maximilian noted their close similarity from the Missouri to the Blackfoot, 384.

horse was quite uniform in the area of its distribution. As a rule, the horses were the property of the man. The woman owned her steed, pack horse, etc., which were usually females, but the herd belonged to the man. When grazing, the horses were usually in charge of boys or young men. At night, the best horses were brought into camp and picketed near the tipis of their owners. No system of branding was used, but each person knew the individualities of his horses so that he could recognize them at sight. Some men had a preference for horses of like color and prided themselves upon being the owners of many white horses, etc. Some mutilation was practised, as colts were sometimes bob-tailed and their ears split, but this was for decoration rather than for identification. Mules were highly prized as they were thought to have superior powers of various kinds. Their origin was regarded as mysterious.

Sleds and Snow Shoes. There seem to be no traditions of using sleds though other tribes and Canadians were known to have used them. The nearest approach to such modes of transportation, appears to have been the dragging of cripples about the camps on sheets of rawhide. Children used the same device in coasting. Grinnell states that the sled was scarcely seen south of parallel 50, the travois taking its place below this line in the Missouri-Saskatchewan area.[1] Exception must be made, however, of some of the village Indians.[2]

According to our information, snow shoes were not in general use except among some of the northernmost bands. In the accounts of war parties, we often heard it stated that the men waded in snow up to their waists.

Caches. To a people often on the move, the cache was indispensable. War or hunting parties often placed in reserve extra ammunition, moccasins, tobacco, dried meat, etc., in pits. A hole about four feet in depth and of sufficient size was dug, lined on the sides and bottom with stones and closed with a heavy slab of the same material, the whole concealed by a covering of earth. Should the party be separated, a straggler would open the cache and take what belonged to him, leaving the remainder for their rightful owners. However, food was seldom cached in this manner because rodents and other animals smelled it out and burrowed into the store. To meet this difficulty various expedients were resorted to. Dried provisions in a parfleche were sometimes hung in a tree near the trail along which a party expected to return. A safer method was to climb a tree beside a young birch, lean it over and tie the parfleche to the top. Rattles of hoofs or deer-claws were tied on to frighten small climbing animals. It was the belief of some, that

---

[1] Grinnell, (d), 156.
[2] Maximilian, 345, states that dog sledges were used by the Mandans.

gun powder rubbed over the package would have an analogous result. Again, food tied in rawhide bags was concealed in hollow trees. Fresh meat was sometimes tied to a stone and anchored under water. When in a rough country, holes in high ledges of rock were used, the opening being securely stopped with stones.

SHELTER.

At present, the Blackfoot erect small rectangular houses of heavy poles, fitted with doors and windows and heated with stoves. Of course, the general architecture and arrangement suggests white influence. These houses are used in midwinter, but during the greater part of the spring, summer and autumn, the people live in canvas-covered tipis, or conical tents, supported by a simple framework of poles. So far, no one except Grinnell[1] has given a detailed description of the structure of a Blackfoot tipi, or for that matter of any tipi, which is strange, to say the least, for this object is one of the most striking characteristics of the roving buffalo hunting tribes.

The Tipi. The poles of the Blackfoot tipi as it stands to-day are long, slender and straight, usually of pine or spruce. They are carefully selected, cut and hauled home from the foothills of the mountains, then peeled of their bark, set up as a frame for a tipi and left to season. A set of well-seasoned poles is looked upon as a valuable asset and is not to be parted with for trifles. As the tipi is made and owned by the woman, it is she who cuts the poles and prepares them, though her husband, if an old man, may lend a hand.

To put up the tipi, a woman unrolls the cover — always folded many times on its vertical axis and finally rolled up. When unrolled its folded form gives the stretch from the base to the smoke hole. Then four poles of about equal length are selected, two of which are laid side by side near or on the folded cover. The other pair are placed across these near the top at a distance from their buts equal to the length of the folded cover (Plate VI and Fig. 60). One end of a thong about 15 feet long is passed around the crossing as shown in the drawing and tied with a simple knot. The poles are then raised and oriented; pole

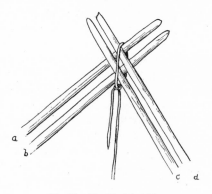

Fig. 60.   The Blackfoot Tie.

[1] Grinnell, (e), 650.

a and *b* toward the east (Fig. 60), *c* and *d* toward the west, the transposition of *b* and *c*, serving to lock the tie so firmly that there is no possibility of slipping.[1] When in place, these four poles rest at the corners of a rectangle, the shortest side toward the east.   (There is some variation in this manipulation, for some women tie three poles and force the fourth under the cord while others tie the four at once.   In Plate VI two poles are laid side by side and a third pole across them).   The remaining poles are now put in place.   These are laid in on the north and south sides of the pyramidal frame, the number on each side being approximately the same; then the poles on the west side, except the one for the middle.   The last thing is the placing of the poles on the east side.   Here the two door poles are placed last and hence rest in a secondary crotch formed by the crossing of the other poles (Plate VI).   All the poles are now in place save three.

The cover is then placed on the frame.   At the top of the cover are two cords (Fig. 61).   These are tied to a pole so that the lower edge of the cover will just touch the ground.   The pole is then ended up and placed at the middle of the west side of the frame (Plate VI).   This pole rests against the main crossing of the poles and extends out through the crotch of the two door poles, or those put in place last, forming a kind of secondary crossing or tripod, standing over the main framework[2] (Plate VI).   The cover is then carried around and pinned together above and below the door. To reach the upper pin holes in a large tipi the woman formerly stood on a travois frame, leaned against the tipi like a ladder; but now a small ladder is often carried for this purpose.

As the tipi stands now, it is much too steep and the cover hangs loose and in folds.   The woman goes inside and adjusts the poles by moving them out and in until the cover is tight and assumes its true conical shape.   She puts the finishing touches to this from the outside, reaching under the cover and making such changes in the positions of the poles as may seem necessary.

There remain two poles.   These are to support the large projecting "ears" at the top.   Standing on the ground, the woman pokes the small end of the pole through a hole, or eye, in the tip of the ear.[3]   The edge of the cover is staked down around the edge.   This completes the process, a task which the average woman will perform in thirty minutes or less.

Formerly, tipis were covered with buffalo skins, soft dressed without the hair.   Twelve to fourteen skins were regarded as necessary to the making

---

[1] Pole *c* is carried over to fall in line with *a*.

[2] Occasionally the use of the three-pole foundation, to be described later, is used by the Blackfoot [Wissler, (a), 7.] By an error of observation this was taken as the typical method, whereas later investigation proved it extremely exceptional and certainly intrusive. The former statement, therefore, stands corrected.

[3] See myth, Vol. 2, 133.

of a tipi cover, though the number varied with the size of the tipi. They were fitted into each other in the most economical way and sewed with sinew. The Museum collection contains two skin tipi covers and two of canvas. As practically all tipi covers are now of canvas, note will first be taken of this type. Spread upon a flat surface the two covers are as outlined in Figs. 61 and 62. The dotted lines indicate the seams where the strips of

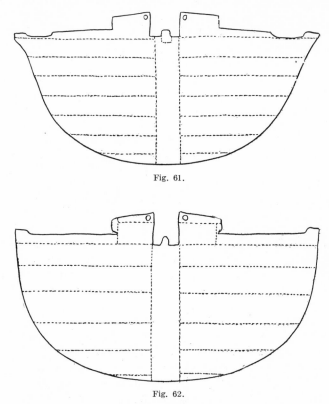

Fig. 61.

Fig. 62.

Figs. 61–62 (50–4485, 4535). Patterns of Canvas Tipi Covers.

canvas are joined. A vertical strip of canvas serves as the foundation, or base, upon which the sides are built and from this the strips of cloth extend at right angles. The "ears" and additional strips for the laps and the sides of the door are added. A small extension is added at the top to which cords are attached for binding to the back pole by which the cover is raised into place (Plate VI). Holes are made in the tips of the "ears" for the ends of the two outside poles. Between the "ears" and the door and also below the door are small holes made in pairs for the pins. Fig. 62 provides for eight pins; Fig. 61 for fifteen pins. Around the curved edge are numerous loops of canvas or other strong cloth. There are fifty of these for the cover in Fig. 62.

From the drawings, it is apparent that the curve of the two tipi covers is not the same, nor do they appear to be the segments of circles. Yet, when a tipi is in position this curved edge describes an approximate circle on the ground. However, the deviations from a true circle on the spread out cover may be more apparent than real, for the geometric centre would naturally fall at the crossing of the poles. A small deviation will also result from the fact that the rear of a tipi is usually steeper than the front.

The cover for the two skin tipis is shown in Fig. 63, the dotted lines indicating the seams where the pieces of skin are fitted together. Naturally, the skins are not laid down in the same manner as the strips of cloth, but a close examination of the drawings shows some resemblance. Down the middle from the top, we find a long narrow rectangular section similar to the foundation strip of canvas, except that it does not extend the entire length. From this radiate the skins trimmed to fit the space. One gets the impression that three skins are placed on each side of the central strip and taking these as a core, six are arranged to give the general curved outline. The manner of attaching the ears and the narrow strip along the lap is similar to the treatment in the canvas cover.

The curved edges are provided with holes for stakes and the laps with holes for the pins. The corners of the "ears" have holes for their supporting poles. A flap is provided for tying to the back pole. The edges of the "ears" and the space between them are notched and two thongs interlaced near the edge, extending from one pole-hole around to the other. The ends of these extend from the small flap and are used to tie the back pole. These are doubtless to support the heavy poles thrust through the ears.

Just below the ears in most tipi covers are strings for tying on the inside to take the strain from the pins. In Fig. 63 there are also strings on the inside, just over the door, for the same purpose.

It will be observed that the shape of the skin cover differs from that of the canvas type. While the laps of the latter are parts of the same straight line, those of the former, deviate from such a line, approximately, 16°. Also, the curve is practically the segment of a circle, in case of Fig. 63, as inscribed from a point near *o*. An examination of the position of the cover when in place on the poles, shows that this centre will fall about at the crossing of the poles.

In how far the canvas type of cover may have been devised in response to the character of the material and in how far this may have influenced the arrangement of materials in the particular skin covers described above, cannot be determined. Fig. 63 was made about thirty-five years ago, the other about ten years ago. The latter, however, was made by an old woman who certainly made skin covers, or at least lived when such were common among the Blackfoot. The inference would be that these skin

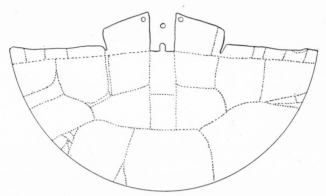

Fig. 63 (50–3835).   Pattern of a Skin Tipi Cover.

covers were made after the prevailing type. The fact that they are similar in detail supports this inference, since according to our information they were not made by the same woman. In general, it may be said that all the Blackfoot tipi covers approximate a semi-circle and their size may be indicated by the following table:—

	Radius.
Specimen.	
Skin cover (3835)	18 ft. 3 in.
Skin cover (4521)	17 ft. 1 in.
Canvas (4485)	18 ft. 7 in.
Canvas (4535)	13 ft. 10 in.

Our information as to how the shape of the tipi cover was secured in its construction is not satisfactory. It seems that the skins were pieced together in the approximate shape. It was then folded and a pair of tipi poles arranged across it somewhat as in Fig. 60; then the edges were trimmed to one of the poles and the ears adjusted. The bottom was trimmed after the cover was in position as in a finished tipi.

The number of poles varies greatly. The writer chose seven tipis, ranging from the largest to the smallest, in the camp circle at a sun dance with the following result:—

Tipis.	Poles.
2	13
1	15
2	16
1	18
1	23

According to Hector and Vaux the number ranges from thirteen to thirty-two.

That the number of poles bears no fixed relation to the tipi is supported by the fact that size is estimated by the number of skins used in making the cover. In general, however, the larger the cover, the greater the number of poles and likewise the greater the variation in their number. The length of pole also varies for tipis of equal size, some projecting several feet above the crossing point, others barely a foot. The poles of a set in the collection are about seven meters in length and about seven cm. in diameter at their buts. The buts are sharpened to prevent slipping on the ground.

The stakes for holding down the canvas are about 42 cm. long, and 2 cm. in diameter, made of birch or choke-cherry wood. The pins are of the same material about 28 cm. long and 1 cm. in diameter. According to observation, the number above the door varies, from six to sixteen, and below the door from two to five. The cover is lapped several inches, the edge on your right as you face the tipi being on the outside, and the pins are usually inserted from the right to the left. When on the move, stakes are usually carried in a bag while the pins were put in a small poke made of soft skin or a bladder precisely as among the Teton.

The door of a tipi always faces the east. It is a long narrow oval opening, sometimes partly cut out but chiefly shaped by use. The lower part is about eighteen inches from the ground and its longest diameter on the specimens in the Museum is about four feet. The opening is guarded by a curtain on the outside, tied by two cords, passing through holes in the cover just above the door. This curtain is distended by a stick crosswise, one near the top and one near the bottom, acting both as weights and as handles in opening the door. In warm weather the door curtain is given a twist and laid over on the side of the tipi. At present, these curtains are made of worn-out blankets or other cloth. So far as our information goes, a rawhide door shaped like and decorated after the manner of a parfleche was sometimes used; but a door curtain made of soft dressed skins seems to have been the usual form. When entering a tipi, one raises the door curtain by the cross stick, puts one foot inside, then stooping over thrusts the head and shoulders through the opening, allowing the curtain to fall behind to its natural position.

Tipis were often provided with door bells. One of the skin tipis in the collection has such a bell, or rattle, made of eight dew-claws from cattle, strung like a tassel, and tipped with pieces of red flannel. This rattle is suspended inside above the door so that any considerable movement of the door curtain or the stretching of the tipi cover as a person creeps through will cause it to swing and announce the intruder. Another specimen in the collection is made of six moose hoofs.

Another interesting part of the tipi is the arrangement for guarding the smoke hole, a large opening in front of the crossing of the poles. This is flanked by two pointed sail-like projections of the cover. By moving the outside poles supporting these "ears" the draught may be regulated and the wind kept from forcing the smoke back into the tipi. At night, when the fire is low, or when rain is falling, the smoke hole may be entirely or partially closed by these "ears." The poles supporting the ears pass through eyes or holes, in their tips and are held in place by strings or small cross sticks tied to the poles.

The inside of the tipi is a circular cone-shaped cavity. The diameter of the base averages about fourteen feet. A general plan of a tipi as seen to-day is shown in Fig. 64. The fire is near the centre, though usually nearer the door than the rear, because the smoke hole is in front of the crossing of the poles. Sometimes the sides of the tipi are steeper in the rear and more sloping toward the front, thereby bring-ing the smoke hole near the centre. The fireplace is a small circle of water-worn stones. Just back of the fire, about half way to the rear of the tipi is a small cleared space upon which sweet grass or other incense is burned from time to time as the ceremonial obligations of the family may require. This "snudge place" may be regarded as the family altar. At the sides toward the rear, are the couches or beds. The usual form is as shown in Plate VII. At the head of each couch is a wooden tripod supporting a back-rest

Fig. 64.   Groundplan of a Tipi.

made of willows strung with sinew (Fig. 12). The beds are several thick-nesses of old blankets laid on the ground, or upon a thin layer of hay. Pillows are used and the sleepers covered with blankets or quilts. The bed on the south side is occupied by the man and woman, small children sleeping on another bed at the foot and larger children, guests, etc., on the opposite side of the tipi. Clothing and similar personal property are kept in bundles or soft bags, tucked away under the sloping edge of the tipi behind the beds where they are out of sight and serve to keep out wind and cold. Cooking utensils and provisions are usually stacked just inside to the south of the door, while riding gear, etc., are stacked on the opposite side.

Most tipis are provided with a back wall, or lining, which is now a pair of blankets or pieces of cloth. In a few tipis one may yet see a single or double back wall of soft dressed cow skins. When a pair of such back walls are used they usually meet in the space between the back-rests, though as may be expected, there is a great deal of variation in their adjustment. They are supported by a thong or rope tied to the successive poles, strings for this purpose being inserted at regular intervals along the upper edge of the back wall. While these are often rendered highly decorative, they are really practical. They serve to keep out the wind and any water that may find its way down the poles from their tops. They protect the people from draughts, as air can enter under the edge of the tipi, pass upward between the cover and the back wall and out over their heads, affording ventilation of the most approved type. There are five specimens in the collection, one of them of buffalo skins, about ten to twelve feet long and six feet wide. They are made of two skins, with a triangular piece extending upward between them to give the whole the proper shape to fit the surface of the conical interior (Figs. 65 and 66).

The space at the rear of the tipi between the back-rests is reserved for ceremonial objects and trophies. These are usually the property of the man. Here will hang from the poles or tripods of the back-rests, the ever present bag for the buffalo rocks [1] and paints (Fig. 42) and the long fringed cylindrical rawhide case for ceremonial regalia (Fig. 43). On the ground, will be found a tobacco board, pipe, pipe stoker, tobacco and a long slender forked stick for picking up coals of fire. The standing and wealth of a family may be gauged by the number and size of the bundles displayed in this place.

While the above detail of the internal arrangement of the tipi applies to the present, it is probably not unlike that of a century ago. The people tell us of a former chief who had a tipi so large that it contained two fires while Grinnell heard of one containing three fires[2], and McDougal visited a very large tipi, containing two fires during the coldest weather.[3] Hector and Vaux saw a few tipis requiring from forty to fifty skins to make their covers, but place the usual number at twelve to twenty. All these were exceptions. Old Indians believe the tipis of their childhood to have been about the size of those now in use. They say that the back-rests were formerly

---

[1] See myth, Vol. 2, 85.
[2] Grinnell, (a), 187.
[3] McDougal, 265.

used in pairs, one for the head and one for the foot of the bed. This was always the case when two or more married men or when two or more wives occupied the same tipi. Enforced monogamy and individualism may account for the present practice. Also, that in large tipis there were often two such beds on the south side and three on the north side. The willow

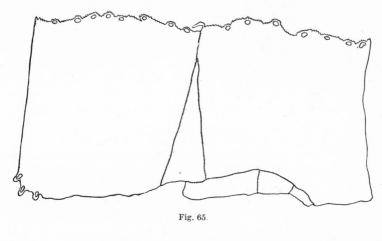

Fig. 65.

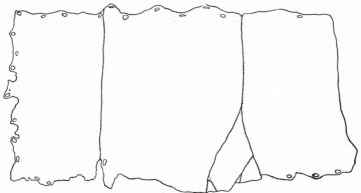

Figs. 65–66 (50–4522, 4521).   Patterns of Back Walls.   Lengths, 3.1 and 3.5 M.

curtains of the back-rests were usually covered with a buffalo calf skin, dressed soft with the hair on and hung by the nose from the top of the tripod. The beds were of buffalo robes similarly dressed, often spread over grass or small twigs with part of a broken tipi pole along the outer edge as a guard rail. The only illumination in the tipi was from the fire, any temporary light being supplied by a brand from the fire. During the winter, or even at any time, the cover of the tipi was often held down by stones laid on its edges. Circles of such stones are to be seen in many parts of the Blackfoot country, marking the sites of former camps or burial tipis.

Grinnell states that according to tradition, the Blackfoot formerly lived in houses made of sticks and mud.[1] According to our information this is an Indian theory rather than a tradition. Their myths and rituals contain no reference to habitations other than tipis. In summer, a sunshade is made of a few poles and a piece of cloth.[2] On festive and ceremonial occasions, a wind brake is set up in the same fashion.[3] One of these may be combined with a tipi so that the onlookers at a ceremony may be sheltered.

Comparative Notes. The cultural affiliations of the Blackfoot in the matter of shelter habits is one of the many interesting problems of the Missouri-Saskatchewan area. So far as we know, no careful detailed study of the shelters of the various tribes has been made and while this is neither the time nor place to make such an investigation, a tentative survey of the area from the vantage of the Blackfoot problem seems necessary to the end we have in view. For many tribes, the necessary data was not to be had, except from the field and we have been obliged to fall back upon the kindness of friends residing on reservations in the area and an objective study of specimens in the Museum collections.

An Omaha tipi cover in the Museum collection is approximately a half circle and is peculiar only in that the "ears" seem to be defined by a slanting cut in the edge. However, when the tipi is up, its general appearance will be about the same as for others. The skins are put together in about the same manner as for the Blackfoot tipi, except that the long rectangular axis is absent. The latter feature seems to be a peculiarity of the Blackfoot. Two native-made models of tipi covers from the Teton have the form of Fig. 63 for the Blackfoot. The "ears" of a Cheyenne model are cut like those of the Arapaho (Fig. 67). In the Teton models they are cut like the Omaha tipi except that they extend out beyond the edges of the laps. There are models of three Sarcee covers in the Museum, all cut on the same general plan, similar to the pattern for Blackfoot skin lodges. The ears are cut like those of the Blackfoot in Fig. 61. Each of these has fifteen poles. An Assiniboine model has a cover similar to the above. The canvas tipis of the Arapaho we have examined do not show the central axis in the pattern, Fig. 67.

[1] Grinnell, (a), 198.

[2] A similar shelter was observed among the Cheyenne, Henry and Thompson, 382.

[3] A similar structure used as a council house by the Dakota is mentioned by Clark, Lewis and Clark, 1, 167.

The poles for the "ears" of the Omaha and Arapaho tipis in the collection do not pass through holes but into little corner pockets. This is true of models from the Cheyenne, Assiniboine and Teton. While from photographs the same appear among the Dakota, Bannock, Ute, Shoshone and according to Grinnell,[1] the Crow also. The Sarcee, on the other hand, have holes in the corners like the Blackfoot: two models in the Museum have poles for the ears similar to those of the Blackfoot, one having cross pieces to prevent slipping too far through the holes, the other having projections formed by trimming away a branch.

According to Dunbar, the Pawnee used but one ear and, hence, one pole, but Grinnell [2] says two were used. In all the photographs of modern tipis that we have seen two ears appear. It is apparent, however, that Catlin's

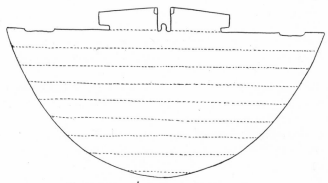

Fig. 67 (50–411a). Pattern of an Arapaho Tipi.

drawings and the implications in Long's narratives to the effect that the Comanche and the Kaskaia (Kiowa-Apache?) used but one ear, must be considered as evidence for an older one-ear type.

Among the Blackfoot, the door faces the east, perhaps because the winds are usually from the west, though a mystic reason is often assigned thereto. This orientation of tipis seems to be usual wherever they are used and not even peculiar to them. The doors for the Cheyenne and Teton models are shaped by a U of bent willow. Henry describes something similar for the Plains Cree, "a piece of hide stretched upon a frame of the same shape as the door, but somewhat larger." [3] Maximilian [4] says a similar thing of the Dakota (Teton?). A similar door with the addition of two cross braces is

[1] Grinnell, (d), 655.
[2] Grinnell, (b), 268.
[3] Henry and Thompson, 513.
[4] Maximilian, 151.

found in the Assiniboine model previously noted. On the other hand, it seems that many of the southern tribes, formerly used a kind of curtain supported on the outside by a pole, serving more as a wind break than a door.

The back wall is used by the Assiniboine at Ft. Belknap, the Gros Ventre, Sarcee and from private information by the Crow and Dakota. A similar contrivance is sometimes seen in the bark and mat covered wigwams of the Menominee and Ojibway. The head of the family sits near the rear on the south side of the tipi among the Dakota, Gros Ventre and Sarcee. As to the custom among other tribes, we have no information. In some cases, the man sits almost opposite the door.

The back-rest was used by the Cheyenne among whom they were usually in pairs and the bed placed upon a raised mattress of similar willow construction. They also seem to have been used by the Gros Ventre, Assiniboine, Cree, Dakota and were no doubt generally distributed. Sketches published by Maximilian also indicate their general use in the earth covered lodges of the Mandan and other village Indians.

According to what may be inferred from the off hand statements of various travelers the number of tipi poles varies among other tribes in much the same manner as with the Blackfoot. The size of tipis seems about the same though Hector and Vaux found those of the Blackfoot larger than those of the Cree and these in turn larger than those of the Stoney Assiniboine.[1]

Passing now to the pole structure of the tipi, we may note that the Blackfoot use of four poles, tied as a foundation, or support, is by no means the rule. So far, we have knowledge of its present use among the Crow, Hidatsa, Sarcee, and Comanche. Long[2] credits it to the Kaskaia (Kiowa-Apache?) but Mr. J. Mooney informs the writer that the Kiowa now use three.[3] On the other hand, we observe that the Teton[4] (Dakota) use three and according to Dunbar[5] the same is true of the Pawnee. The Museum has native-made models of tipis from the Cheyenne and the Assiniboine[6] in which the three pole foundation is used. From other sources of informa-

---

[1] Hector and Vaux, 257.

[2] James, 293.

[3] On a recent visit to the Saultaux, Mr. Skinner found a four pole foundation in use with a tipi-like structure, which is further suggestive of the northern distribution of this type.

[4] The contrary statement of Curtis, Vol. 3, 24, is obviously incorrect since contradictory to his own photographic illustrations.

[5] Clark, 372.

[6] While Clark, in commenting on an abandoned Assiniboine (?) camp, describes tipis as being erected by tying four poles as a support to eight to twelve others, the original statement of Lewis implies that this is the result of observations on the tipi which they used on the expedition, the property of the captive Snake woman (Bird-woman). As this woman was an Hidatsa captive, it is likely that she used the mode of the Hidatsa and Crow. The probability of this is increased by information from Gilbert L. Wilson that when the Mandan and Hidatsa used tipis they employed the four pole foundation.—Lewis and Clark, 1, 285, 310.

tion [1] we may add the Gros Ventre, Arapaho, Kiowa, and Nez Perce. Carver [2] states that two were used by the Sioux and Henry [3] says the same thing of the Cree, though it is not clear whether this means two pairs of tied poles or actually two poles. However, recent information from the Eastern Cree, furnished by Mr. Alanson Skinner, makes it probable that this refers to two tied poles, supported by a third crotched pole; hence, a three pole foundation.

The Blackfoot mode of setting up the poles seems to differ greatly from that used with the three pole foundation. We observed the following procedure among the Teton:— The cover of the tipi is laid out, folded in half and three poles laid upon it, two parallel and the other crossing between them at the proper place. This is so that the proper height of the crossing may be taken. These poles are tied at the crossing by the end of a long strap or thong. When set up, these poles form a tripod, one leg of which is to be on the left side of the door. The two rear legs of the tripod are nearer together than they are to the forward leg. Poles are then laid in, on the left of the door pole and then on the right. Two turns of cord are made by walking around the poles twice (usually to the right) and the end tied down to the forward leg of the tripod. The rear poles are now put in place. The pole for the cover is often the longest and may bear a scalp-lock at the end. The cover is tied to this and raised in place, after which the cover is pinned above the door and staked down. The poles are so adjusted that the back of the tipi is usually steeper than the front. According to Dunbar, the Pawnee take the turns with the cord after all of the poles are in place. Among the Teton and Assiniboine, as well as the Blackfoot, the end of this cord is often fastened to a stake in the centre of the tipi to prevent the wind from overturning the structure.

A model from the Northern Cheyenne has the appearance of a faithful copy of a tipi. The poles are arranged as a tripod, one leg to the left of the door, as among the Teton, around which are nine other poles. The whole arrangement of the poles is like that of the Teton. However, all the poles except the one by which the cover is raised, are bound by the cord. An Assiniboine model is similar to the above in construction, except that the forward leg of the tripod is to the right of the door. Mr. Reese Kincaide kindly furnished the following additional information from the Cheyenne:— "The third pole of the tripod always forms the left side of the door as one enters the tipi, so they begin to fill in with the balance of the poles to the

---

[1] Messrs. James Mooney, Reese Kincaide, W. C. Roe, J. R. Walker, R. H. Lowie and H. J. Spinden.

[2] Carver, 231.

[3] Henry and Thompson, 513.

right of this one, then to the left and last at the back.   When all the poles are in place, the long end of the rope is wrapped several times around the tops of the poles to bind them securely together, and tied to the north tripod pole, or to a stake near the centre of the tipi floor, if the wind blows hard. As to the Arapaho women, I find that their way is exactly the same as that of the Cheyenne.   Their tipis differ in shape from those of the Cheyenne in that the base diameter is less in proportion to the height than with the Cheyenne.   As one Cheyenne woman said, 'We want our tents big.'   To the uninitiated they both look alike, but the Arapaho tipi is the more pointed of the two."

From the foregoing accounts it is evident that the appearance of the crossing of the poles and the tops of tipis among the Teton, Assiniboine, Arapaho and Cheyenne will differ from the Blackfoot and Crow.   With the former, the two door poles in the upper crotch are not in evidence as they are the first poles in position.   Familiarity with the forms produced by these two kinds of foundation, enables us to make use of photographs as a check on other information.   Those at hand, agree with the above, except in case of the Kiowa where they seem to have the form of the four-pole foundation.   True, a three pole foundation can be so manipulated as to give the appearance of the other type; but experiment will show that to do so implies a four-pole beginning, in reality a four-pole foundation.   The difference between the two types may be characterized by the fact that in the four pole type the door posts are the last to be placed, whereas in the three pole type they are the first.

Fig. 68.   The Assiniboine Tie.

The tops of the Blackfoot and Sarcee tipis are often characterized by very long poles, though there seems to be too much variation in this to be distinctive.   This peculiarity is especially noticeable in Crow tipis.

In the course of this comparison, some data as to the tie for the foundation poles came to hand.   The Crow used the tie and same manipulation of the poles as the Blackfoot, according to a series of photographs taken by Rev. O. A. Petzold.   The Assiniboine tie, as it appears in a model in the Museum [1] is shown in Fig. 68.   The ends of the thong are drawn home with a simple knot, the essential feature being the peculiar passing of the thong around the poles.   In the sketch, *a* is the

---

[1] Collected by Mr. Tappan Adney.

door post. The Teton tie is as follows:— "Lay three poles side by side. Pass one end of a rope under all the poles at the place to tie (Fig. 69). Then pass it over the third pole, under the second, over the first, under the first, over the second, under the third, over the third and once around all. Then draw on the rope, bringing the poles into a triangular relation, and tie (Fig. 69). Then wrap the long end of the rope about one of the poles. To set up the poles spread the three tied poles to equal distances, drive a peg into the earth, and tie the long end of the rope to it. Then lean ten or more poles against the tripod. In old times, the tripod pole that was to be next the door was longer from the tie to the ground than the

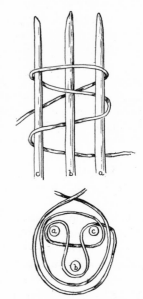

Fig. 69. The Teton Tie.

others, so that the side of the tipi opposite the door was more nearly perpendicular than the other." [1]

The Cheyenne and Arapaho tie is not so complicated as the preceding. As tipis usually face the east, we may designate the legs of the tripod as north, south and east. Referring to Fig. 70, the tie is as follows.— "Take the north and south poles and lay them side by side in front of you, pointing from you and towards the left, the south pole being nearest you. Now take the east pole, or the left door post, and lay it across the other two, having the part below the tie a little longer than for the others. Then take the cord, passing it, not around as some do, but up and down at the crossing point,

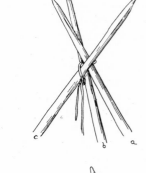

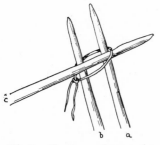

Fig. 70. The Cheyenne and Arapaho Tie.

[1] Dr. J. R. Walker.

the rope being between the one and the two.   Then tie, bringing the knot on the under side, or so it will be down when the tripod is set up.   Draw the rope fairly tight.   Now, set up the tripod with the one pole to the east, pull the south pole in that direction and the other one towards the north, spreading them as much as the cover requires." [1]

The aim of all tipi ties is to provide a locking arrangement so that the weight of the tipi will only draw the cord tighter.   While with the Blackfoot four-pole tie, this is easily accomplished by passing the rope once around as in case of the Cheyenne and Arapaho tie, raising them into position and spreading; the result is attained with three poles only by the careful manipulation of the poles from the starting position.   On the other hand, both the Teton and Assiniboine ties, the latter being a simpler mode of the former, lock in the most efficient manner conceivable.   Unfortunately, we have no more data but the preceding seems to show that the Siouan peoples fall into one type as opposed to the Blackfoot, Cheyenne and Arapaho.

The general import of the discussion, so far, seems to be that the tipi of the Missouri-Saskatchewan area is, excepting a few very minor details, of one definite type — crossing poles on a three or four-pole foundation, a one piece cover, an oval door, two ears for the smoke hole, etc.   Its absolute distribution is fairly well known.   There is, however, one aspect of its use so far given little consideration.   Among the Blackfoot it was the primary, indeed, the only shelter, winter and summer alike.   On the other hand, the Hidatsa and other village Indians used the tipi but occasionally when on a summer hunt or otherwise out from their more permanent home.   Between these extremes there were all degrees of alternation.   We may, therefore, for convenience divide the tipi users into two groups: one in which the tipi was the primary dwelling and one in which it seems secondary.   Among the former, may be counted the Blackfoot, Crow, Assiniboine, Sarcee, Gros Ventre, Plains Cree, Cheyenne, Arapaho, Kiowa, Teton and Yankton Dakota, Comanche and perhaps the Wind River Shoshone and some Ute.   To the other class belonged the Hidatsa, Kansas, Mandan, Omaha, Osage, Otto, Ponca, Santee Dakota, the Northern Shoshone, Nez Perce, the chief modern divisions of the Caddoan stock, possibly some Cree and some Central Algonkin tribes.   While it is true that most of these latter were to varying extents agriculturalists, this may have no particular significance other than geographical position; yet, in most cases such a use of the tipi can be correlated with a temporary migration out across the open country to hunt buffalo.   Within the historic period, at least, the tipi and the horse, with all the appurtenances thereto, were the prerequisites of such movements.   In a

---

[1] Mr. Reese Kincaide.

general way, the popular conception that wherever the buffalo, the horse and the tipi were found together, all the main material cultural characteristics of the area were in function, was not far from the truth among those tribes using the tipi as a primary dwelling.

There is, however, another point to be considered. No matter how nomadic these tribes were in summer, they tended to fixed abodes in the winter. This was more marked in the north than in the south, and while the tipi when the primary shelter seems to have sufficed for the winter in most cases; it is not certain that any of these tribes were entirely ignorant of wooden shelters. Catlin [1] states that the Blackfoot, Crow and Assiniboine, in winter, pitched their tipis in thick timber, always found in the valleys and sometimes built rude huts there. The same, according to our field-notes, was stated by the Teton. The Blackfoot now seem to believe that skin tipis were superior in winter for warmth and comfort. Elsewhere, it has been shown that while the Santee Dakota used houses of stakes and bark, such were summer dwellings near their fields and that the greater part of the year, especially in winter, they lived in tipis. Further, J. O. Dorsey makes it clear that among the Omaha, tipis were used in winter as opposed to earth covered and other houses in summer. Thus, "The tent was used when the people were migrating, and also when they were travelling in search of buffalo. It was also the favorite abode of a household during the winter season, as the earth lodge was generally erected in an exposed situation, selected on account of comfort in the summer. The tent could be pitched in the timber or brush, or down in wooded ravines, where the cold winds never had full sweep. Hence, many Indians abandoned their houses in winter and went into their tents, even when they were of canvas." [2] Curiously enough, the Skidi (Caddoan) claim to have used the tipi exclusively before taking up the earth covered house.[3] This is a subject deserving special investigation for, if it should turn out that the earth covered and other forms of shelter are, in the main, truly secondary in this area a problem of very great importance would be defined.

This is not the place to follow up the suggested primary nature of the tipi as a dwelling among these tribes and the clues to its possible origin; yet, it seems worth while looking toward the north for related types. A good description of the Chippewa tipi has been given by Beauliew.[4] Three poles are set up in a tripod and the other poles arranged around them. The cover is of birch bark. The interior is fitted with a floor of fir or cedar boughs

---

[1] Catlin, 1, 43.
[2] Dorsey, 271.
[3] Dorsey, G. A., xiv.
[4] Clark, 375.

and a cross pole to support the kettle. The Museum collection contains two models of similar tipis from the Ojibway of Leech Lake, Minnesota. The pole structure of these is braced by one or two horizontal poles bent around and bound to the other poles by strips of bark. Around the frame is stretched a broad band of birch bark. This bark cover is usually rectangular in shape, instead of semicircular as with the true tipi. In the north, the present Athapascan groups, or Dene, use a tipi somewhat like that of the Ojibway, though the horizontal poles are usually lacking. In some cases, true tipis, with two ears, are to be seen.[1] Yet this tipi, whether covered with skin or bark is often like the Ojibway in that the cover is rectangular and rests low on the frame; being, in other words, more of a wind-break.

According to Willoughby,[2] a tipi-like house was used occasionally in New England, especially by the Penobscot. As this is, in some respects, a part of the northern Algonkin area, it may be assumed that this form is allied to that used by the Ojibway and Cree. The Nenenot of Labrador spend the entire year in a tent of skins which according to Turner's description has the general form of a tipi but not the characteristic cover, door or ears.[3] The internal arrangement is much like that for the Dog Rib and Beaver Indians. This is particularly true as to cross poles above the fire. The Eskimo about Bering Strait, according to Nelson,[4] use a conical summer tent but its structure is less like the tipi than the tents of the Nenenot. In the Museum, there are models of tipi-like structures, covered with birch bark, from Siberia, but the principles of their construction are unlike those of the American tipi.

Morice [5] states that the Beavers live in skin covered conical tents all the year round. Four poles are first set up, supported by forks at their ends, around which other poles are arranged in a circle. Over this is drawn a cover lapped over the door, like a tipi. Even the door curtain is distended by two cross sticks as among the Blackfoot. The smoke hole is guarded by one ear supported by an outside pole. A conical structure sometimes covered with skins, with a single ear, supported by a pole, and a door curtain, crossed by a stick at the lower edge, was sometimes used by the Thompson Indians,[6] also a floor covered with fir branches similar to that used by the Beaver, Dog Rib and Nenenot.

Thus, from Labrador to the Thompson Salish of interior British Columbia, we find a similarity in the internal arrangement of the general tipi-like

---

[1] Russell described a Dog Rib tipi that has two ears supported by two outside poles.
[2] Willoughby, 118.
[3] Turner, 299.
[4] Nelson, 260.
[5] Morice, (c), 192.
[6] Teit, 197.

structure. Among the Dene generally, and some of the Salish, there is a tendency to use a four-pole foundation and one ear for the smoke hole. The former characteristic we have found among the Blackfoot, Sarcee, Crow, Mandan, Hidatsa [1] Comanche and perhaps the Kiowa-Apache; the former northern Plains tribes in historical times, the two latter regarded as spending at least part of the year near the Black Hills at the opening of the historic period. The use of one ear seems to have disappeared in the historic period. Yet Hector and Vaux [2] speak of Blackfoot tipis with two ears as if that were different from what they had observed to the eastward, and previous reference to Long and Catlin implies that one ear was formerly used by the Comanche and Kiowa. In a way, this reënforces the four-pole tribal distinction, placing their geographical group in a class with tribes on the northern border, differentiating them from a southern and eastern three-pole group in which the Dakota are the most conspicuous.

It was not intended that this comparative review should be complete but sufficient to give basis for a suggestive statement. It appears that the tipi-like structures of the Beaver, Chippewa and Dog Rib Indians tend to one type while those of the buffalo hunting tribes tend to another. We designate these types as northern and southern, respectively. Both have many things in common, but such are general rather than specific features. There are suggestions that a few specific features of the northern tipi were formerly found in the Missouri-Saskatchewan area, among the Sarcee, Blackfoot, Crow, Comanche and perhaps the Kiowa and Kiowa-Apache. If, as has been assumed, the latter of these tribes formerly roamed in Montana and northward, we are tempted to look to the Dene and northeastern Algonkin areas for the centre of distribution for this type. However that may be, we may conclude with having shown ground for differentiating the tipi of this area from similar types of shelter used elsewhere and that while the Blackfoot and some of their neighbors conform in most respects to the southern type, they also show correspondences with the northern type.

---

[1] The fact that the Hidasta and Mandan are credited with but occasional use of the tipi, and that of the Crow type, need not be taken into account here; though more information is desirable. Maximilian credits the Hidatsa with having formerly roamed about like the Crow, living chiefly in tipis.

[2] Hector and Vaux, 257.

DRESS.

Satisfactory data as to original costume is scarcely to be had as no one now living can remember the time when some commercial cloth was not in use. We have, however, some descriptive notes by Henry and Maximilian. According to the former, the young men, at least, were not over-dressed, appearing at his post nude on several occasions, apparently much to his disgust. However, this must be taken with some reserve since to reach the post these young men swam their horses across a stream, a circumstance naturally justifying nakedness.[1] Yet he is quite specific in the following:—

"They wear no breech-clouts and are quite careless about that part of the body. Their dress consists of a leather shirt, trimmed with human hair and quill-work, and leggings of the same; shoes are of buffalo skin dressed in the hair; and caps, a strip of buffalo or wolf skin about nine inches broad, tied around the head. Their necklace is a string of grizzly bears claws. A buffalo robe is thrown over all occasionally." [2]

Again he writes:—

"The ordinary dress of these people is plain and simple, like that of all other Meadow Indians; plain leather shoes, leather leggings reaching up to the hip, and a robe over all, constitutes their usual summer dress, though occasionally they wear an open leather shirt, which reaches down to the thigh. Their winter dress differs little from that of the summer; their shoes are then made of buffalo hide dressed in the hair, and sometimes a leather shirt and a strip of buffalo or wolf skin is tied around the head. They never wear mittens. * * * * The young men have a more elegant dress which they put on occasionally, the shirt and leggings being trimmed with human hair and ornamented with fringe and quill work; the hair is always obtained from the head of an enemy." [3]

A description by Maximilian may be added to make the picture more complete:—

"The dress of the Blackfeet is made of tanned leather, and the handsomest leather shirts are made of the skin of the bighorn, which, when new, is of a yellowish-white colour, and looks very well. A narrow strip of the skin with the hair is generally

---

[1] In this connection, the following note by Henry has some comparative interest:— "They wear not the least article of covering; therefore, during their stay, which is generally most of the day, they remain perfectly naked, walking or riding about the fort with the greatest composure. Some of them have modesty enough to use their hands to cover the parts, while others find means of putting it into the body, and then fastening the orifice so tight with a string that scarcely anything appears." Henry and Thompson, 544). As the same mode of concealment is depicted in some of Catlin's drawings it seems likely that this custom was generally diffused throughout the area.

[2] Henry and Thompson, 525.

[3] Henry and Thompson, 725.

left at the edge of such a skin. These shirts have half sleeves, and the seams are trimmed with tufts of human hair, or of horsehair dyed of various colours, hanging down, and with porcupine quills sewn round their roots. These shirts generally have at the neck a flap hanging down both before and behind, which we saw usually lined with red cloth, ornamented with fringe, or with stripes of yellow and coloured porcupine quills, or of sky-blue glass beads. Some have all these fringes composed of slips of white ermine; this is a very costly ornament, these little animals having become scarce. Many of the distinguished chiefs and warriors wore such dresses, which are really handsome, ornamented with many strings hanging down, in the fashion of a Hungarian tobacco pouch. When these leather shirts begin to be dirty, they are often painted of a reddish-brown colour; but they are much handsomer when they are new. Some of these Indians wear on the breast and back round rosettes like the Assiniboins, but this is only a foreign fashion, and the genuine Blackfoot costume has no such ornament. Their leggins are made like those of the other Missouri Indians, and ornamented, in the same manner, with tufts of hair or stripes of porcupine quills; the shoes, of buffalo or elk leather, are also adorned with porcupine quills, each having a ground of a different colour for its ornaments; thus if one is white, the other is yellow — a fashion which does not exist lower than the Missouri, where both shoes are of the same colour. The chief article of their dress, the large buffalo robe, is, for the most part, painted on the tanned side, but less skillfully than among the other nations. In general, there are black parallel lines mixed with a few figures, often with arrow heads, or other bad arabesques; others, again, are painted with representations of their warlike exploits, in black, red, green, and yellow. The figures represent the taking of prisoners, dead or wounded enemies, captured arms and horses, blood, balls flying about in the air, and such subjects. Such robes are embroidered with transverse bands of porcupine quills of the most brilliant colours, divided into two equal parts by a round rosette of the same. The ground of the skin is often reddish-brown, and the figures on it black. All the Missouri Indians wear these robes, and it is well known that those of the Manitaries and the Crows are the most beautifully worked and painted. In the description of Major Long's first expedition, there is a representation of such a skin, but it is the only one of this kind which has come to my knowledge, and I have, therefore, had a drawing made of such a one. The Company gives the value of six to ten dollars for such a skin. During the summer, the fur is worn outside, and in winter inside. The right arm and shoulder are generally bare. It might be thought that this dress was too hot in summer, and too cold in winter, but custom reconciles us to everything, and they dress pretty nearly in the same manner in the opposite seasons." [1]

The present people claim no knowledge of a time when breech cloths were not used by the men, as Henry's statements imply. On the other hand, the usual accuracy of this observer must be given some weight. His remarks from time to time, give one the feeling that a simple apron may have been worn in front like the Assiniboine and some other tribes. On the other hand, the Blackfoot visiting the Missouri in Maximilian's time are credited with having the body covered most of the time in contrast to other tribes to the east and south.[2] This is further supported by the almost entire

---

[1] Maximilian, 248.
[2] Maximilian, 247.

absence of body painting.   Thus, notwithstanding Henry's statements, our information and that of other observers would characterize the Blackfoot as more completely clothed than most other tribes of the area.

Men's Suits.   A man's shirt collected by Mr. Grinnell may be taken as the Blackfoot type.   The body is made of two deer or antelope skins, joined by a seam at the top except across the slit for the head.   The skin from the hind legs of the animal forms side trailers as shown in Fig. 71, and that

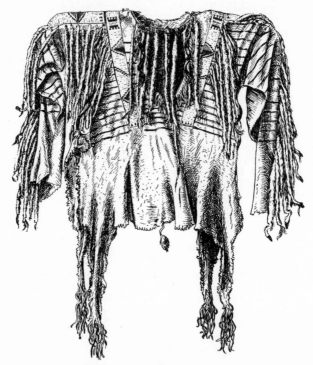

Fig. 71 (50–1681).   A Man's Shirt.   Length, 84 cm.

from the tail with a tuft of hair remaining forms a centre border ornament. The back of the body is a duplicate of the front and the sides are open save for two ties, one near the arm pit, the other at the waist.   The sleeves are closed: one is made of a single piece, the other of two pieces.   It is thus possible to make such a garment of four pieces, cut from two patterns as shown in the sketch.   All the open edges of the body are cut into short broad fringes.   The tips of the trailers are cut into fringes of twenty centimeters, the strands of which are twisted.   The ornamental effects of these are further increased by the hair remaining on the part from which they were cut.   The cuff is split back some distance and the edges of each half notched with points instead of the rectangular fringes of the body.   Beaded bands are laid over the shoulders and down the sleeves.   There are four of these bands, or two pairs; those over the shoulders bear an even number of the main design units, those on the sleeves, an odd number.   The neck slit is bordered before and behind by a triangular flap, one half red, the other black, so arranged that the one in front will have the red on the right side of the wearer.   This flap is decorated with fringes.   The upper part of the body and the sleeves are painted red with cross bands of black.   Along

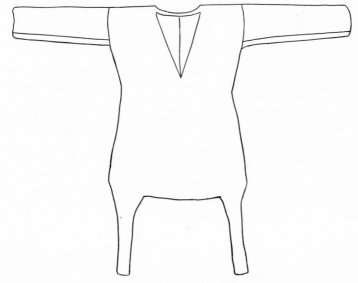

Fig. 72.   Pattern for a Shirt.

the tops of the sleeves and across the shoulders are strips of white weasel. skins.   Usually, the making of each strip requires a complete skin to furnish the black tail tip, making a garment quite expensive.   Six tassels of red horse-hair are symmetrically arranged among the weasel strips.   As the two sides of this shirt are alike, it can be worn either way.   There is no vertical open-ing as on the bosom or back of trade shirts; but the head slit can be enlarged or reduced by a lace on the shoulders.

Another shirt in the collection is generally similar to the preceding, though not so well made.   It bears, however, a typical feature not found on the preceding; viz., a large beaded disk on the breast and back.   Taking shirts as they come when observed at a tribal gathering, these disk ornaments prevail and the native opinion seems to be that they should appear on all decorated shirts.

A shirt of calf skin is made on the same general pattern. The tails, however, are square cut and the edges plain. Instead of weasel skins, the sleeves, back and front are bordered by very long fringes of calf skin. Another shirt is similar in pattern, but decorated with bands of porcupine quill work with fringes of weasel skins and human hair.

The two former may be taken as the highest type of man's shirt, and also the most characteristic. The two latter appear to represent an intrusive type since the decorations are almost identical with some observed among the Assiniboine. The same resemblances hold for the beading and quill technique. In passing, it may be noted that the punctured shirt known to the Nez Perce and elsewhere is occasionally met with among the Blackfoot.

With such shirts, the men wore long leggings reaching to the hip and supported from the belt by a strap. The type is shown in Fig. 73. The bottoms are usually cut into four parts and notched or slightly fringed. Bead or quill worked bands extend almost the full length of the leggings and are bordered by strips of weasel skin or other fringes. As a rule, leggings are painted yellow and striped with black throughout, similar to those of the Mandan and other village Indians; yet the cut of the Blackfoot legging differs at the ankle, those of the former being full and trailing.[1]

Fig. 73 (50–1683). A Man's Legging. Length, 92 cm.

Suits for small boys were often made on the same lines, one in the collection being in most respects a duplicate of that just described. While in popular literature, garments with weasel skins are regarded as the insignia of a chief and there are some traditions to that effect, it may be doubted that such a rule was strictly observed. As nearly as we can judge from the data at hand, it is rather to be considered full dress.

---

[1] Maximilian, 341.

During trade days many men wore large overcoats made of blankets. These had closed sleeves and usually an attached hood. A few of these were still in use in 1905. The breech cloth is still worn by old men. It passes between the legs and under the belt behind and before. The pendant ends are cut square but do not hang far down like the long pendant ones of some Siouan tribes. In former times, these cloths were of deer or other soft skin. One in the collection is a rectangular piece 31 by 138 cm. The belt is of similar material, 5 by 140 cm.

Robes of buffalo skin were in general use but these have been displaced by trade blankets. Though robes are now made of steer-hide, these are seldom worn, being reserved for bed covers or decorative purposes. According to Grinnell, winter robes of beaver skin were in use, and summer robes of cow and other skin from which the hair had been removed.[1] The collection contains an elk hide robe tanned on both sides, one of which bears painted designs. The man's robe was usually crossed by a broad band of quill or beadwork, examples of which may still be seen attached to trade blankets. There are several such bands in the collection. One which may be taken as the type is quill worked (Fig 74). The most characteristic

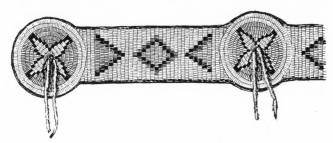

Fig. 74 (50–6787).   Part of a Blanket Band.   Length, 154 cm.

feature is the use of disks, usually four in number, to the centres of which strips of weasel skin are attached. These bands were placed upon the tanned side of the buffalo robe, extending from the head to the tail. In use on trade blankets, they are worn horizontally: i. e., passing around the waists of the wearers. As to how they were worn in the past, there is a difference of opinion: some maintaining that they were vertical on the back, as among the Arapaho. This is doubtless, equivalent to stating that sometimes the robe was worn with the head uppermost and the tail at the heels, an exceptional position, for it is agreed that the correct position was the head to the

---

[1] Grinnell, (a), 197.

left and the tail to the right.   The painted designs were usually pictographic for men and striped for women, though great variations were permissible. Some maintain that the women wore these stripes transversely, while in men's robes, if used, they were vertical.

Ordinarily, the men drew the robe about the body, almost to the arm pits and secured it by a kind of hitch in front, so that it remained in position. The trade blanket is still secured in this manner.

Headgear.   To quote from Grinnell:— "Women seldom wore a head covering.   Men, however, in winter generally used a cap made of the skin of some small animal, such as the antelope, wolf, badger, or coyote.   As the skin from the head of these animals often formed part of the cap, the ears being left on, it made a very odd-looking headdress.   Sometimes a cap was made of the skin of some large bird, such as the sage-hen, duck, owl, or swan." [1]

There is some recollection among the Piegan of the rawhide eye shade, painted like a parfleche, used by the tribes beyond the mountains.   This seems not to have come into general use and to have been regarded as a borrowed custom.   With the shirts previously described, a special head-dress seems to have been worn.   This consisted of a hood of cowhide falling low down on the neck, covered completely with strips of white weasel skins. To the top, a pair of horns were attached.[2]

The feather headdress used by many tribes seems not to have found favor among the Blackfoot.   In fact, what the eagle feather seems to have been in the costume of other tribes, the weasel skin was to them.   It should not be inferred, however, that there were no associations in which eagle feathers were of prime importance.

Another type of headdress was made of strands of human hair, joined by pieces of gum.   This was hung from the back of the head.   There is a fine specimen of this type in the Museum, attributed to the Nez Perce and we have seen others among the Gros Ventre.   Catlin observed something of the kind among the Crow and in the Museum there is a Shoshone piece made of buffalo hair.

Special forms of headdress are associated with ceremonies and therefore belong to another part of our subject.   In general, however, they are of one type, a head-band to which the accessories are fastened.

Collars and Mittens.   Skins of otter, fox, coyote, etc., were split in the middle, slipped over the head and worn over the breast and back.   These were, however, hung with charms and so must be regarded as not strictly articles of dress.   Bead-covered cords were worn in parallel curves across

---

[1] Grinnell, (a), 196.
[2] Catlin, 1, Plate 14, 32.

the breast by men.   In recent years, at least, mittens of buffalo skin were used.   Each was joined to the sleeve by a cord so that it might not be lost.

Women's Suits.   Women's costumes were not given much consideration by Henry so that the following quotation from Maximilian must suffice:

"The dress of the women is the same as among the other Missouri Indians; it is a long leather shirt, coming down to their feet, bound round the waist with a girdle, and is often ornamented with many rows of elks' teeth, bright buttons, and glass beads.   The dress wraps over the breast, and has short, wide sleeves, ornamented with a good deal of fringe, which often hang down nearly in the same manner as in the national Polish dress, but not below the elbows.   The lower arm is bare.   The hem of the dress is likewise trimmed with fringes and scolloped.   The women ornament their best dresses, both on the hem and sleeves, with dyed porcupine quills and thin leather strips, with broad diversified stripes of sky-blue and white glass beads. * * * * * The girls are dressed in the same manner as the women, and their dresses are generally ornamented with elks' teeth, for which the Indians pay a high price."[1]

Grinnell states that

"The ancient dress of the women was a shirt of cowskin, with long sleeves tied at the wrist, a skirt reaching half-way from knees to ankles, and leggings tied above the knees, with sometimes a supporting string running from the belt to the leggings. In more modern times, this was modified, and a woman's dress consisted of a gown or smock, reaching from the neck to below the knees.   There were no sleeves, the armholes being provided with top coverings, a sort of cape or flap, which reached to the elbows.   Leggings were of course still worn.   They reached to the knee, and were generally made, as was the gown, of the tanned skins of elk, deer, sheep, or antelope."[2]

If this is correct as to the older form, these people had a costume somewhat like the tribes farther north and eastward and it would imply that the later form of dress was an intrusion from the Missouri area.   This may, however, refer to the Cree type to be mentioned later.

The Audubon collection contains a woman's dress dating back to about 1843 (Fig. 75).   The structural details of this agree with examples of recent make collected by us.   Pieces of elk or deer skin are cut as shown in the pattern (Fig. 76).   The spreading parts to form the cape are pieced out with a long strip cut as shown.   To this often adheres the tail tuft, as for shirts, and a fringe of hair on the edges.   The pendant points, also in the hair, are fringed and twisted as for shirts.[3]   However, the tail may be a part of the skirt piece.   The top of the yoke is joined to the skirt piece by overlacing, the edge being slightly notched or fringed.   In the completed garment these two halves of the robe are sewed together across the top,

---

[1] Maximilian, 249.
[2] Grinnell, (a), 196.
[3] See drawings by Catlin.

except at the neck-hole. The sides are sewed to the arm pits, except for mothers of nursing children when the sewing stops at the breast. The lower part of the skirt may be pieced if the original tanned hide is not large enough and likewise a strip may be inserted at the side. The bottom is cut zigzag with a point at each side and one in the middle. The side edges are fringed as is also the bottom.

Double pendant thongs are placed across the skirt at intervals in two

Fig. 75. A Woman's Dress. Length, 133 cm.

or three rows. Sometimes these are anchored to bits of red and black cloth, encircled by beads. At each side below the first row of fringes a small cloven hoof-shaped piece of skin is attached (four in all). Still lower, appears a triangular piece, half black and half red, and two rectangular pieces similarly divided. Duplicates of these appear again on the back.

The beading on the yoke is still much like that on the Audubon specimen, consisting of rows of tubular glass beads, following the contour of the cape, and curving around the tail tuft.   Below this beading were hung elk teeth;

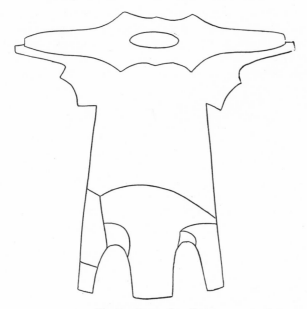

Fig. 76.   Pattern for a Dress.

now shells, thimbles and other trinkets.   In former times, quills were used in place of beads.   There are no sleeves, the cape hanging freely over the bare shoulders and arms.

Women's leggings are now usually of cloth reaching the knee.   They have a single seam on the side, worn on the outside of the leg.   When decorated, a beaded piece of tanned skin, about 14 by 25 cm. is placed at the bottom, the edges overlapping and held by a series of two strand laces by which it may be drawn snug to the ankle (Fig. 77).   The high upper of the moccasin is gathered beneath this so that the legging reaches to its decorated border.   The combined legging and moccasin of southern tribes was not used.   The beaded designs are usually arranged to give a striped effect.

Fig. 77 (50–4498).
A Woman's Legging.
Length, 43 cm.

Belts.   Belts were worn by both men and women, but especially by the latter.   It is said that those of the men were very narrow, but otherwise similar to those used by women.

At present, women wear belts of trade leather about 10 cm. in breadth,[1] decorated with beads and brass nails.   One very old piece that we collected is covered with many heavy brass buttons; this was said to have been the only form of belt decoration in former years and as the buttons were costly, such a belt was a luxury indeed.   Some of these belts seem to have borne the long trailers found on Assiniboine belts.

Women's knife cases were similar in construction to the belts and were suspended by a cord so as to hang down on the thigh.   For men, however, the belt passed through a hole in the margin of the scabbard, as observed among the Assiniboine.

Moccasins.   The moccasins seem to have been of two general forms. The one, which is the older by tradition, is made from a single piece cut as shown in Fig. 78.   The following note of explanation is contributed by Mr. William C. Orchard:— "That part of the pattern marked *a* forms the upper side of the moccasin; *b*, the sole; *e*, the tongue, *f*, the trailer.   The leather is folded lengthwise, along the dotted line, the points *c* and *d* are brought

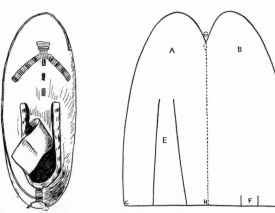

Fig. 78 (50–4411).   The One-piece Moccasin Pattern.

together and the edges sewed along to the point *g*, which makes a seam the whole length of the foot and around the toes.   The vertical heel seam is formed by sewing *c* and *d* now joined to *h*, *f* projecting.   The strips *c* and *d* are each, half the width of that marked *h*, consequently the side seam at the heel is half way between the top of the moccasin and the sole, but reaches the level at the toes.   As the sides of this moccasin are not high enough for the

---

[1] The almost exact uniformity in the width of the belts collected by us makes it probable that the Blackfoot had a definite standard measure for these.

wearer's comfort, an extension or ankle flap is sewed on, varying from two

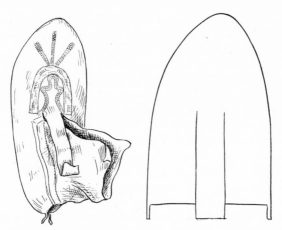

Fig. 79 (50–4566).   Pattern of Upper for a Hard Soled Moccasin.

to six inches in width, cut long enough to overlap in front and held in place by means of the usual draw string or lacing around the ankle."

Fig. 80 (50–4406). A Blackfoot Moccasin. Length, 27 cm.

Winter moccasins were of this form, but usually made of buffalo skin with the hair inside. The moccasin generally worn to-day is of two or more pieces and usually provided with a rawhide sole. Parfleche and bags are often pressed into service for such purposes, remnants of the painted designs being observable within. The soles conform generally to the outlines of the foot and are in consequence rights and lefts. The uppers are of the form shown in Fig. 79. Sometimes the tongue is joined instead of being continuous with the material of the upper. Around the ankle on many moccasins is a fold of cloth, usually red, bordered by black or green and ornamented by a peculiar cross stitch [1] (Fig. 80). A high top is frequently added which, with the tongue, fully covers the ankle. The string or lace, passes around under the fold of cloth, occasionally looped through the heel, making the entire cir-

---

[1] In former times, it is said, a strip of white weasel skin was attached to the moccasin of a prominent man.

cuit. Sometimes, however, two strings are used, the ends fastened near the heel seam, but otherwise as before.

Trailers are used. Thirteen pairs of Blackfoot moccasins examined by us ranged as follows: no trailers, 4; one trailer, 3; two trailers, 3; fringed along the heel seam, 3.

No definite differences between moccasins used by men and women are now observable. In summer, a plain canvas moccasin is the usual form for ordinary use. For decoration, paints, quills and beads are employed. As among many other tribes, the entire decoration of the upper is completed before attaching to the sole. This joining usually begins at the toe with the parts turned wrong side out but righted before entirely sewed up. The use of tiny rattles of metal or dew-claws as moccasin decorations seems not to have found a place in Blackfoot culture. At one time, it was fashionable for men to fasten the tails of badgers or other objects to the heels as trailing ornaments, a practice formerly observed among the village Indians. Nothing of this kind remains, though a few old men still tie tails to their stirrups — apparently a survival.

Hair Dress. The women wear their hair in two braids, or hanging loose, confined by a band about the forehead. In either case, it is carefully parted in the middle. The braids are used by girls and matrons, while old women almost invariably wear the hair loose. This is also the usual form for ceremonies. In careful dress, the hair is smoothed down closely over the sides of the head and temples concealing the ears, though generally exposing more of the forehead than is the case among the Dakota and some other tribes. The hair is seldom dressed with paint though it may have been otherwise in the past, for Henry says, "Their ornaments are few — feathers, quillwork and human hair, with red, white and blue earth, constitute the whole apparatus; but they are fond of European baubles to decorate their hair. The young men appear proud and haughty, and are particular to keep their garments and robes clean. The women are a filthy set. Their dress consists of leather; their hair, never combed except with the fingers, is worn loose about the neck and always besmeared with the red and lead-colored earth. This gives them a savage countenance, though the features of many of them would be agreeable, were they not so incrusted with earth." [1] Grinnell seems to confirm the carelessness of the women in hair dressing.[2] While at present this characterization is not just, allowance must be made for changes introduced by the schools and otherwise.

In contrast to the preceding, the men seem to have given a great deal of

---

[1] Henry and Thompson, 525.
[2] Grinnell, (a), 197.

attention to the hair. Henry states, "The young men allow theirs to flow loose and lank about their necks, taking great care to keep it smooth about the face; they also wear a lock hanging down over the forehead to the tip of the nose, these cut square, and kept smooth and flat as if to hide the nose." Again, "The elder men allow their hair to grow, and twist it in the same manner as the Assiniboines; but instead of forming the coil on the crown, they wear it on the forehead, projecting seven or eight inches in a huge knob, smeared with red earth." [1]

The long face-lock is not now seen but will be noticed in some of Catlin's drawings. Maximilian gives the following:— "Their hair hangs down straight and stiff, often in disorder over the eyes and round the head. Young people, however, who pay more attention to neatness, part it regularly over the forehead, and comb it smooth.* * * * Some braid the hair in a long thick queue behind, and many, especially the medicine men or jugglers, wear it, like the Mandans and Minitaries divided into several thick queues all around, and generally bind them all together with a leather strap, in a thick knot over the forehead." [2] The knot referred to has long been the characteristic of a medicine pipe man.[3] Occasionally, the hair on the top of the head is cut short and dressed to stand on end. However it may have been in the past, many men of the present spend a great deal of their time brushing and caring for their hair. They admire long hair and use charms to increase its length. (Plates II and VII.)

Like other Indians, the Blackfoot had a distaste for face-hair. While a few old people can recall a few instances in which men of their tribe trained small beards, they were the exceptions. The pubic hair and that of the arm pits is fairly abundant and some individuals are very hairy on the back and limbs. All such hair save that of the pubes, where concealed by the breech cloth, is usually pulled out with tweezers. Formerly, tweezers are believed to have been made of wood or bone.

Combs. So far as known, true combs were never in use, their place being taken by the widely distributed porcupine tail brush. Three types were collected by us. The type known to most tribes in the Missouri valley, a porcupine's tail mounted on a stick, was in general use. In Fig. 81, we see a true brush, porcupine bristles bound to a stick by rawhide. An unusual form made by binding horse hair is shown in Fig. 82. Sometimes brushes were made by binding a bundle of small flexible twigs instead of hair or bristles.

---

[1] Henry and Thompson, 525.

[2] Maximilian, 247.

[3] For a photograph showing this type of hair dress we are indebted to Mr. Walter McClintock, Plate II.

Hair and Neck Ornaments.   We may finally direct our attention to hair ornaments: though we shall very soon find ourselves led into charms and amulets, a subject not within the scope of the present work.   At present, there are few, if any, native hair ornaments.   The bunches of feathers and other objects tied upon the head are survivals of an immediate past in which they had a value other than decorative.   According to Maximilian [1] a small shell was often suspended over the temple: again, small locks wrapped with brass wire (evidently a detached ornament) hung from one or both sides of the forehead.   The use of eagle feathers on the head seems much less pronounced than among the Dakota, the inclination being to use strips of ermine and bunches of owl feathers.

A peculiar necklace worn by some men is formed of fungus, prized be-

Fig. 81.   Fig. 82.

Fig. 81 (50–4546).   A Hair Brush.   Length, 11 cm.
Fig. 82 (50–15).   A Hair Brush of Horse Hair.   Length, 9 cm.

cause of its delicate odor.   It consists of variously shaped pieces about the size of tennis balls, strung at intervals on a thong.   In former times, bear's claws were worn as among many neighboring tribes.

Tattooing and Mutilation.   While tattooing was not a custom, it was occasionally performed.   The designs were simple, confined to the arms and face.   They were pricked by needles and colored with gun powder. Nose rings, as well as lip, cheek and ear plugs seem to have been unknown. The ears of children are pierced, but the ear ornaments worn at present are simple.   They are usually rectangular or circular pieces of shell secured in trade.   While perhaps more women than men wear these ear ornaments, there seem to be few important differences between them.   It is said that

---

[1] Maximilian, 247.

formerly, small rings of buckskin were worn, though not to the exclusion of shells. The ears of infants are usually pierced by old women. Formerly, a sharpened twig, usually of service berry, was thrust through the lobe and broken off close to the surface. At present, a piece of lead is used. An open ring, something like that used for hogs' noses is formed and pressed home on the part to be perforated. The irritation at the points of contact and subsequent pressure forms an opening. Head deformation was not practised. Scarification was rarely seen;[1] though it was sometimes an incidental result of sacrifices to be described in a future publication. We found no traces of mutilation of the genitales as observed by Henry and Maximilian among some of the tribes of the Upper Missouri valley. The name of a Piegan band, however, refers to a similar malformation of the women.

Pigments and Painting. The use of paint for the face is still a daily practice with many and seems to have been universal in former years. Henry credits them with ten pigments:— "The ten different colors of earth and clay they use in painting and daubing their garments, bodies, and faces are: a dark red, nearly a Spanish brown; a red, inclining to pale vermillion; a deep yellow; a light yellow; a dark blue; a light or sky-colored blue; a shining and glossy lead color; a green; a white; and charcoal." [2] The probability is that some of these were secured in trade. The following kinds of native paints were listed by us. As these will be fully treated under the ceremonies in which they find their most important function we give the English equivalents of their names here:—

Yellow earth.

Buffalo yellow (buffalo gall stones).

Red earth (burned yellow earth).

Red earth (as found).

Rock paint (a yellowish red).

Many-times-baked-paint (a yellow earth made red by exposure to the sun).

Red many-times-baked (a similar red, as found).

Seventh paint (a peculiar ghastly red-purple).

Blue (a dark blue mud).

White earth (as found).

Black (charcoal).

We have not had an opportunity to submit samples of these native pigments for analysis nor have we verified by observation the sources and conditions given in the above table. It is quite probable from the above, that

---

[1] Maximilian, 247.

[2] Henry and Thompson, 731.

the term for blue is also used for green. The claim is made that a native green was often produced from a mud; but that this was in reality a green in the modern sense of the word is unlikely. The reader should not confuse this list with dyes, for by paints we mean the equivalent of the Indian term for face and body paint. While, naturally, these pigments may be used for other purposes, it is as articles for the toilet and especially as ceremonial accessories that they find their true functions. As we have here to do with the former, to the exclusion of the latter, we may be content with their enumeration. Henry in his contemptuous way observes:—

"The Slave Indians, [Blackfoot, Sarcee and Gros Ventre] daub their bodies, robes, and garments profusely with red earth, which appears to be the principal article of their toilet. They have another favorite pigment [Our seventh paint], which they procure on their excursions beyond the rocky mountains, of a glossy lead color, which is used to daub their faces after red earth has been applied. This kind of paint tends to give them a gastly and savage appearance."[1]

Maximilian gives the following account as observed in his day:—

"They paint their faces red with vermilion; this colour, which they procure by barter from the traders, is rubbed in with fat, which gives them a shining appearance. Others colour only the edge of their eyelids, and some stripes in the face, with red; others use a certain yellow clay for the face, and red round the eyes; others, again, paint the face red, and forehead, a stripe down the nose, and the chin, blue, with the shining earth from the mountains which I have before mentioned, and which, being analyzed by Professor Cordier, at Paris, he found to be mixed with an earthy peroxide of iron, probably mixed with some clay. Others colour the whole face black, and only the eyelids and some stripes red. The women and children paint the face only of a uniform red."[2]

At present, men as well as women paint the face, usually with ordinary red pigment of their own finding. It may be applied wet or the face rubbed with tallow into which some of the pigment is worked with the hands. Sometimes the backs of the hands are painted. The women often trace the part of the hair with vermillion. The making of designs, stripes, or the use of two or more colors is practically limited to ceremonial functions. However, one frequently sees a person with large circular spots of red on the cheeks, a broad band on the forehead and chin, but with such irregular outlines as to preclude their interpretation as true designs. In this statement, we refer to ordinary every day painting and not to that directly associated with ceremonies.

Paint pouches have been considered in another part of this publication. A toilet outfit can scarcely be distinguished from a ceremonial outfit as both

---

[1] Henry and Thompson, 525.
[2] Maximilian, 247. The shining earth mentioned here seems to be our "seventh paint."

are found in all degrees of completeness. The ideal outfit for all uses is a series of bags containing the different kinds of paint, a bag containing pieces of tallow, a few clam shells for mixing (though a cup is usually called into service nowadays) and a few pointed sticks used in penciling some of the more elaborate designs in ceremonial painting.

Some of these pigments are still used in decorating rawhide bags, drums, tipis and robes, though commercial colors are much preferred. In former times, the paint was applied and rubbed into the texture with wedge-shaped pencils of bone. The collection contains a set of five cut from the spongy end of a buffalo leg-bone. We have been informed that the pointed toe bones of buffalo and deer were sometimes used in the same way. At present, rags and trade brushes are often used. Formerly, the outlines for such painting were traced with a marking bone. This was a knife-shaped piece with a smooth rounded point. In use, the point was heated in the fire and applied to the rawhide with pressure, where it left a depressed and often a colored trail. The same method was used in robe decoration. At present, this technique is rarely employed, trade crayons being more convenient. Stencils are frequently used in tipi decoration, but this seems to be a recent intrusion.

Comparative Notes. To place the Blackfoot as to their dress we must give a general review of the distribution of the related types. The earlier observers show a tendency to make the man's shirt with fringes of hair, etc., bearing quill ornaments and especially the rosette, or disk, an Assiniboine characteristic. Of the Mandan, Maximilian says, "These Indians generally wear no covering on the upper part of the body; the leather shirt of the Assiniboins, Sioux [Dakota], Crows, Blackfeet, and other nations that live more to the north and north-west, are seldom used among them; yet a few individuals have obtained them from those Indians, either as presents, or by barter."[1] Brackenbridge observed such shirts occasionally among the village Indians of the Missouri.[2] From all the information at hand, it seems probable that the Hidatsa, Arikara and Mandan, made little use of the shirt as a regular costume, if indeed, they used it at all.

The men's shirts in the Museum collections seem to have the following characteristics:— The Arapaho specimens have closed sleeves like a modern coat with seams at the sides of the body. One specimen, however, has one side open, held together at intervals by a tie. Among the Gros Ventre specimens there is a ceremonial shirt with a half sleeve; i. e., closed from the elbow to the wrist-but open at the sides of the body like Dakota shirts. The shirts of the Dakota, as just mentioned are open at the sides; many times not even

---

[1] Maximilian, 340.
[2] Brackenridge, 150.

tied, and in most cases provided with half sleeves. The Nez Perce specimens are open at the sides and also provided with what appears to be a half sleeve, though the opening in the sleeve is very small. These Nez Perce shirts resemble those of the Blackfoot in that the tail tufts are at the bottoms of the skirts.

Shirts seem not to have been used by the men among the Osage, Pawnee, and in Long's time among the Kiowa, Cheyenne, Arapaho and Comanche.[1] However, the Arkansas seem to have used shirts.[2]

The general type to which the Blackfoot specimens belong: i. e., the fringed front or sleeves, with broad decorative bands over the shoulders and on the sleeves, was used by the northern Shoshone, the Sahaptin, Crow, Assiniboine, Dakota, and probably by some of the village tribes of the Upper Missouri. For later years, this list could be much extended as any collection of photographs will show. Like the Blackfoot, the northern Shoshone and Sahaptin show a tendency to use the closed sleeve, but with a fringe confined to the upper arm, a feature not usually observed east of the Mountains. Henry describes the Cree shirt as having sleeves open from the shoulders to the elbow like those of the women.[3] Maximilian says something like this of the Blackfoot.[4] From the data at hand, it appears that this decorated shirt is a special costume, or a kind of regalia, with predominant military associations. Its general diffusion among southern non-shirt wearing tribes is apparently due to this idea. It seems to have been most accentuated among the Dakota, Assiniboine, Crow, Blackfoot and their immediate neighbors west of the Great Divide and by the hair fringes and otherwise varying devices symbolic of military triumphs.

So far as our positive information goes, the people wearing shirts as a regular costume were the Assiniboine, Blackfoot, Nez Perce, some Shoshone and interior Salish, Crow and possibly the Dakota and Gros Ventre. Bearing in mind that the Cree and eastern Dene wore shirts, we may confidently look upon this as a northern characteristic. Hence, it may be correct to say that as a true garment for men, the shirt was not a characteristic of the entire area; but a special shirt worn on dress occasions, was quite characteristic, at least, during the historic period. Naturally the Blackfoot with their immediate neighbors show strong tendencies toward the use of both types.

In like manner, the woman's dress or shirt, has a special distribution. The general type of Blackfoot sleeveless dress was used by the village Indians,

---

[1] James, 3. 48.
[2] Marcy, 98.
[3] Henry and Thompson, 514.
[4] Maximilian, 248.

the Crow, Dakota, Arapaho, Nez Perce, northern Shoshone, Assiniboine, and Plains Cree.   From collections of photographs it appears that the same form of dress is found among the Ute, Kiowa, and Comanche.   At an earlier period, it seems that the Assiniboine women wore dresses like the Cree.[1] What this garment was is not quite clear though it has been described by Mackenzie,[2] Henry[3] and Harmon.[4]   All are agreed that the sleeves are detached and closed from the wrist to the elbow, "but thence to the shoulder they are open underneath and drawn up to the neck, where they are fastened across the breast and back." [5]   Harmon says they are held on by a cord joining the two sleeves.[6]   Mackenzie says the corners of the open part of the sleeve hang down behind the waist.[7]   The dress proper was fastened over the shoulders by strips of leather, "a flap or cape turning down about eight inches, both before and behind, and agreeably ornamented with quill-work and fringe." [8]   (Curiously enough, the women of the area wore their robes with a fold at the top).   This cape seems to correspond in a way with the yoke to the Blackfoot dress just described.   Otherwise, the skirt of the Cree and Assiniboine is apparently similar to the characteristic dress of the present Plains women.   The closed, or partially closed sleeve, seems to be a northern characteristic as Carver states that the women seen by him wore no sleeves.[9]   Recalling Grinnell's statement as to older Blackfoot costume having sleeves, we may conjecture that his informants had the Cree type in mind.

Among some of the Algonkins and the eastern Siouan tribes, the women wore skirts reaching to below the knee, which were simply pieces of cloth or buckskin open on one side or in front.   Long[10] observed this among the Osage and again when among the Cheyenne and other tribes.[11]   Something like this seems to have been anciently worn by the Ojibway and Eastern Cree.   If we take the more general form, of a short skirt reaching from the waist to below the knees, we may add the Pawnee.[12]   In these cases, an upper garment was worn, usually without sleeves, cut square with a simple hole for the head, or a kind of cloak fastened over one shoulder.   These characteristics serve to differentiate this type of woman's dress from that of the tribes previously enumerated.

---

[1] Henry, 306; Henry and Thompson, 517.
[2] Mackenzie, xciv.
[3] Henry and Thompson, 514.
[4] Harmon, 275.
[5] Henry and Thompson, 515.
[6] Harmon, 176.
[7] Mackenzie, xciv.
[8] Mackenzie, xciv; see Maximilian's Atlas for drawings.
[9] Carver, 229.
[10] James, 1, 119.
[11] James, 3, 47.
[12] Clark, 156.

The western Dene women seem to have inclined toward the apron and robe [1] of the Pacific shore, while the interior Salish appear to have used a form intermediate between the Dene and the Blackfoot type.[2]

Thus, it appears that the general type of woman's dress in the Missouri-Saskatchewan area was distinct from that used to the north, east and south. It was, however, common to many parts of the Sahaptin and Shoshone areas. This dress seems to be primarily a one piece garment as opposed to that used by women in other parts of the continent. Within its area of distribution, it seems possible to differentiate certain sub-types. The Sahaptin seem to have a tendency to make a true sleeve of the cape extensions, strongly suggestive of the detached sleeves of the Cree. The Kiowa, Comanche and possibly the Ute tend to the use of a low-cut open neck, as in the sleeveless waists of the Pima, Moki, etc. Again, these more southwestern tribes seem to have to used a detached cape, to all appearances a duplicate of the large yoke in Dakota dresses. Some collectors have, however, given these capes a ceremonial value.[3]

The specimens of women's dress which we have examined give the Arapaho and perhaps the Cheyenne a tendency toward a yoke with square cut cape extensions; the Dakota have a characteristic notched cape, though Catlin sketches them as in the Blackfoot mode. Early observers regard the Assiniboine as in appearance scarcely to be distinguished from the Cree of the Plains and while no clear description of costumes of that period have come to hand, Maximilian's artist sketches Assiniboine women with a dress strongly suggestive of the Cree sleeved type. Thus, from the pattern alone, the Blackfoot are nearest the Mandan and other village Indians. While this is not the place to enter into a discussion of the embroidery and other decorations it may be said, that the Sahaptin and the Northern Shoshone seem to be of the exact Blackfoot variety, while the Dakota form is found among the Kiowa, Arapaho, Ute, etc. In practically all the specimens examined, we have found the U-shaped turn, which on Blackfoot dresses borders the tail tuft. We feel that the Blackfoot form can be safely taken as indicating the real origin of this decoration, notwithstanding the symbolic character given it by some tribes.

It would be interesting to follow up the problem as to the more specific origin of the Blackfoot form of dress. From structural and geographical points of view, there must be a historical relation between the inserted top piece of the Blackfoot yoke, the attached cape-like yoke of the Dakota, etc.,

---

[1] Harmon, 244.

[2] Hill-Tout, 68; Teit, 215.

[3] Battey, 128. Also a mixed blood Piegan once showed the writer a similar cape said to have been used by nude women dancers among the Blackfoot; all our other informants denied this, however.

and the folded over yoke of the Cree. The separate cape of some Shoshone and other southern tribes may be accounted for as a special differentiation or an independent feature afterward entering into the dress. While we need more data, the distribution is suggestive; the separate cape in the south, the heavy combined cape and skirt in the middle, the lighter more sleeve-like cape in the north. Grinnell's statement that the Blackfoot women formerly used a costume that we now know to have been typical among the Cree and Saultaux, implies that among them the widely distributed Plains type is intrusive.

The woman's legging seems to have been the same for the Cree,[1] Assiniboine, northern Shoshone, Mandan, Hidatsa, and Dakota. This type may be characterized as the short ankle to knee type.

One type of legging worn by women and also by men seems to have been in occasional use among most tribes in this area, but also very widely distributed among the Algonkin and other eastern tribes. This type may be characterized by a stiff flap along the outer seam produced by an extension of the two edges of the cloth or leather beyond the seam. The distribution of this type is so wide and its use outside of the area so varied, that it cannot be considered important from an ethnographic point of view. The most probable thing seems to be that here it is an intrusive eastern type, not by any means displacing what seems to be a type peculiar to this area.

In general, the cut and make of clothing was uniform among the eastern and southern neighbors of the Blackfoot. As Catlin states, "I cannot say that the dress of the Mandans is decidedly distinct from that of the Crows or the Blackfeet, the Assinneboins or the Sioux; yet there are modes of stitching or embroidering, in every tribe, which may at once enable the traveller, who is familiar with their modes, to detect or distinguish the dress of any tribe. These differences consist generally in the fashions of constructing the head-dress, or of garnishing their dresses with the porcupine quills, which they use in great profusion." [2]

Blackfoot costume, in contrast to the Crow, presents a dark ground due to the mode of dressing deer skins.[3] This peculiarity, while not unknown among other Plains tribes prevailed among the Shoshone and especially among all the Plateau and Mackenzie tribes from whom it may be assumed to have reached the Blackfoot.

The following comparative study of moccasins is contributed by Mr. William C. Orchard. It appears that the types fall into three classes: *a*, those with separate soles; *b*, the soles and uppers of one piece, *c*, the boot

---

[1] Henry and Thompson, 514.

[2] Catlin, 1, 100.

[3] Catlin, 1, 45.

moccasin. Since the former seems to predominate west of the Mississippi River, it will be considered first.

Pattern No. 1, Fig. 83, may be called a three piece pattern, consisting of upper, tongue and sole. A cut of about three inches down the centre of the upper is made to a point just below the instep and short cut at right angles to that, making a T-shaped cut with the vertical line much longer than the horizontal. To the edge of the short cut is sewed the tongue. (With Ute moccasins it is to be noted that the tongue is sewed to the three edges made by the horizontal cut). The upper is sewed to the rawhide sole turned inside out. When the sewing is completed the moccasin is turned right side out; consequently the stitches are on the inside as is invariably the case with the stiff soled moccasins. The common form of lacing (Fig. 100) is used to secure the moccasin to the foot. In most cases, the top of the moccasin is formed by an extension sewed to the upper.

Pattern No. 2, Fig. 84. The shape of the cut in this case causes the heel seam to be made on the inner side of the foot. In other respects it is the same as No. 1.

Pattern No. 3, Fig. 79, is a very simple pattern for a two piece moccasin. The upper and the tongue are cut in one piece from soft tanned leather. In many cases, the edges of the tongue are cut parallel; but occasionally taper toward the end which consequently increases the height of the moccasin at the heel. In the majority of cases an extension or ankle flap has been added and the common method of lacing employed.

Pattern No. 4, Fig. 85, is distinguished by one straight cut down the centre of the upper and an inset tongue with a pointed base. This pattern, almost peculiar to the Ute, is sometimes found without a tongue, a wedge-shaped insert taking its place.

Pattern No. 5, Fig. 86. The upper has one straight cut down the centre of the pattern and a V-shaped cut at the end, forming a very short pointed tongue. This form seems to be peculiar to the Sarcee.

Pattern No. 6, Fig. 87 is peculiar in that the flexible sole is cut wide towards the heel and turned up, forming a seam with the upper tapering down towards the tread of the foot. The cut of the upper is as in No. 1. We have so far observed this among the Shoshone only.

Pattern No. 7, Fig. 88. A cut is made nearly the entire length of the pattern, along the centre. In the opening thus made a long tapering piece of leather is let in, the sewing on either side being carried to a point just over the instep, the loose part of the inset forming a tongue. The pattern is cut four or five inches longer than is required and the pieces extending beyond the heel seam are fringed. So far, this form seems peculiar to the Apache.

The second general type (b) is less frequent than the preceding. What

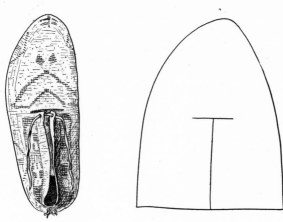

Fig. 83 (50–4405). Moccasin Pattern No. 1.

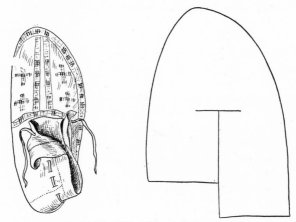

Fig. 84 (50–6462). Moccasin Pattern No. 2.

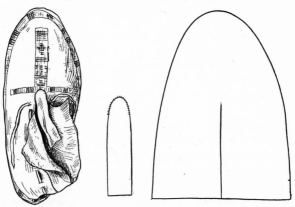

Fig. 85 (50–1278). Moccasin Pattern No. 4.

we may designate as Pattern No. 8 has been described in the discussion of Blackfoot moccasins (Fig. 78). This is, perhaps, the most general form for the one piece moccasin.

Pattern No. 9, Fig. 89. This pattern is folded down the middle from toe to heel and the edges from *a* to *b* are sewed together, forming the toe

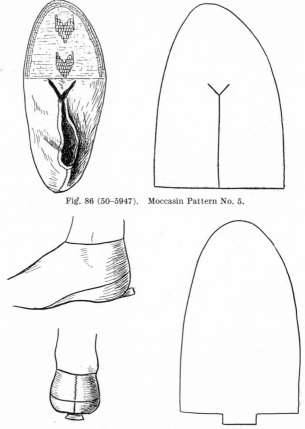

Fig. 86 (50–5947). Moccasin Pattern No. 5.

Fig. 87. Moccasin Pattern No. 6.

of the moccasin and those from *c* to *d*, the heel. Ankle flaps are sometimes sewed along the sides of the opening and in some cases are cut in one piece with the pattern. The seam down the centre of the foot is drawn, or gathered, near the toes in such a manner that the stitches do not go beyond, but end about half an inch from the point of the moccasin on the upper side of the foot. The heel seam being pointed at the lower end, it is sometimes turned in and sewed to the upper in an upright position, giving a somewhat rounded finish to the outside.

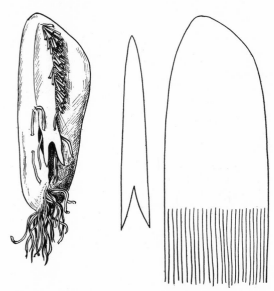

Fig. 88 (1–5423).   Moccasin Pattern No. 7.

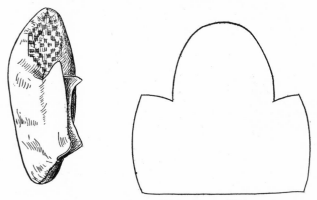

Fig. 89 (50–2251).   Moccasin Pattern No. 9.

Pattern No. 10, Fig. 90. For this pattern, a soft tanned leather is used for the entire moccasin. The edge of the larger piece of leather between the points marked *a* and *b* is sewed to the edge of the smaller piece from *c* to *d*, the larger piece being turned up and gathered. This forms the toe of the moccasin. The two ends marked *e* and *f* are brought together and sewed, which makes the heel seam.

Pattern No. 11, Fig. 91. This type of moccasin is made from a simple

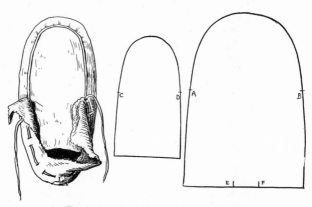

Fig. 90 (16–987). Moccasin Pattern No. 10.

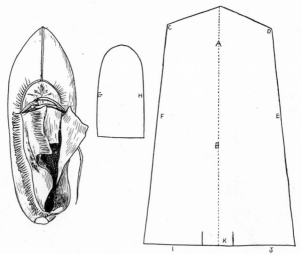

Fig. 91 (1–4614). Moccasin Pattern No. 11.

pattern but the sewing, or bringing together of the parts, is complicated. Two pieces of soft tanned leather are required, consisting of a piece marked *a*, the upper and sole combined; and a smaller piece for the tongue which is inset far enough down the front of the upper to cover the instep. The pattern for the upper is folded along the dotted line and those edges marked *c* to *d* are sewed together after the point produced by the folding, has been trimmed off, which brings the seam down the centre of the foot, under the toes. The inset piece is now sewed into the opening, between that part marked *c* and *d* which is in the centre and the two points at *f* and *e* on either side. The distance along the edge between *e* and *f* being greater than that on the inset piece between *g* and *h* it is overcome by a series of small "gathers" which are remarkable for their regularity and neatness, in some cases each fold being emphasized by a pointed implement. The heel seam is made by sewing the edges *i* and *j* together, the trailer *k*, being cut off, which forms an inverted T-shaped seam.

In most cases, the sides of the moccasins are not high enough and ankle flaps or extensions have been sewed on, from two to ten inches in width. The common form of lacing is employed. There are other methods of finishing the toe seam than those mentioned above. The Naskapi moccasins examined, instead of the seam turning under the toe which is brought about by rounding the point *h*, have a cut at right angles to the seam, thus removing the point and producing a T-shaped seam, the cross arm of the T being above the toes. Among the eastern Cree, a series of moccasins was collected with the extremity of the toe seam gathered in various forms.

Pattern No. 12, Fig. 92, from the Shasta is almost unique. This pattern

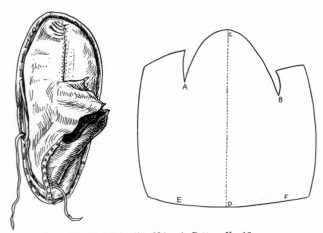

Fig. 92 (50–3442). Moccasin Pattern No. 12.

is folded down the centre from *c* to *d*. The points *a* and *b* are brought together, making the distance from *b* to *c* greater than that from *c* to *a*, which is overcome by a series of gathers made on the longer edge while the seam is being sewed, producing a curved seam from the point of the toe to the instep, the convex side being towards the outer side of the foot. This pattern is for the right foot and it will be seen that the ankle flap on the inner side, is much larger than that on the opposite side. The heel seam which is made between the points *e* and *f* is not sewed the entire length, a space of about 2 inches at the top being left free. The usual method of lacing is employed, the thongs being of sufficient length to wind around the ankle several times.

The boot type of moccasin seems to be a southwestern rather than a northern type. The prevailing type in the Plains is in structure at least, a combination moccasin and legging. This is shown in Pattern No. 13, Fig. 93. The upper is of simple cut, independent of the legging, in somewhat of a horseshoe shape. The legging is a rectangular piece of leather broader at the end which joins to the upper, narrowing slightly at the ankle and gradually growing wider towards the knee, conforming in a small measure to the shape of the leg. The seam is up the front of the leg with a narrow overlooking strip giving the appearance of being fastened on the side. The sole is of rawhide and the sewing of the upper to the sole is performed in the same manner as in sewing moccasins of the first class (a). Occasionally, a draw string, or lace, is used around the ankle.

Pattern No. 14, Fig. 94, observed among the Hopi, is another interesting example. In cutting the pattern a whole hide of soft, white, tanned deer skin is used. An irregularly shaped piece from the neck or leg is used for the toe piece. The only part that is shaped, is that covering the toes and instep, the shaped end forming the tongue. The legging is made of one half the hide, cut down the centre from head to tail, the head end being trimmed to fit around the heel of the moccasin, overlapping the toe piece on either side. The sole is made of rawhide, cut longer and wider than the foot, allowing the edge to be turned up, which is neatly gathered at the toe and heel in the sewing, the stitches being made from the outside. When the toe piece is in place, the legging is sewed on commencing with *a* of the leg piece at *d* on the sole, bringing the cut edge of the hide to the inside of the leg.

The legging effect is produced by a spiral-winding of the hide around the leg, commencing on the inside and winding from left to right across the front of the leg which brings the cut edge of the leather on the outside of the roll. The remaining loose ends are tucked in around the knee and the whole is secured by means of a thong, or strap, sewed to the tail end of the hide.

Pattern No. 15, Fig. 95 is another Pueblo variation. It has a seam at the back of the leg. Soft, white tanned deer skin is used for the uppers and rawhide for the soles. The toe piece *a* is cut separate from the leg, making

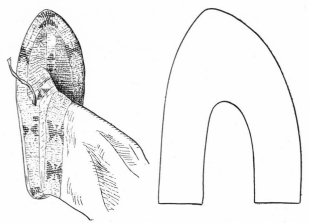

Fig. 93 (50–5739). Moccasin Pattern No. 13.

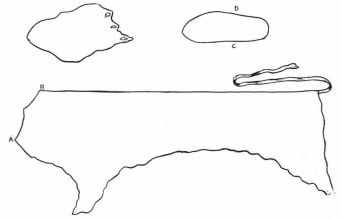

Fig. 94. Moccasin Pattern No. 14.

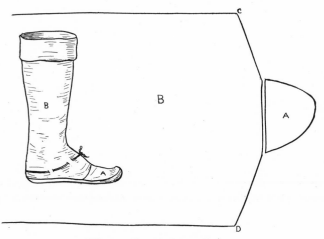

Fig. 95. Moccasin Pattern No. 15.

a seam across the instep.   In sewing the upper to the soles, which are turned up all around, the stitches are made on the outside and the sole leather is gathered at the toe and heel.   The leg is cut of sufficient length to make a fold around the top immediately below the knee.

Pattern No. 16, Fig. 96 is frequently met with among the Apache.   The edge of the upper from *a* to *b* is sewed to the sole, commencing at *c* on the sole and going back round the heel along the inner side of the foot and finishing at *d, b* overlapping *a*.   The dotted line across the toe of the pattern indicates another method of cutting the leather, the toe piece being separate. The dotted line *ef* indicates a shorter cut for the leg.   The sole of the Apache

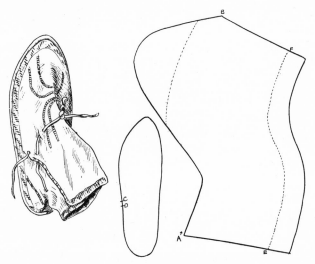

Fig. 96 (1–5173).   Moccasin Pattern No. 16.

moccasin is of thick rawhide and is turned up all round, the upper being sewed to it just clear of the edge, making a projection of varying width according to the thickness of the sole leather used.   The draw string, or lace, is sometimes used around the ankle.   The seam up the legging is buttoned or tied with a short thong.

Pattern No. 17, Fig. 97 is seen among Zuni collections.   It is made of soft tanned leather uppers and rawhide soles.   The sole is turned up about one half to three fourth inches all around.   The upper, at the point marked *a* is first attached to the sole below and a trifle forward of the ankle on the outer side of the foot and carried around the heel along the inner side of the foot around the toes and back to the starting point, with that part of the upper marked *b*, overlapping that marked *a*.   The leather of the sole at the

toes and heel is gathered with fine stitches which are made on the outside.
A triangular piece, *c*, is sewed to the upper at *b*, reaching well to the back
where a button is used to secure the moccasin to the foot.

Pattern No. 18, Fig. 98 is similar to the preceding.   The toe piece (*a*)

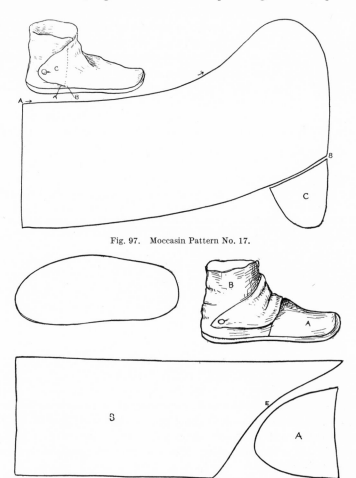

Fig. 97.   Moccasin Pattern No. 17.

Fig. 98.   Moccasin Pattern No. 18.

is cut separate from the rest of the upper (*b*) from a piece of soft tanned skin.
The sole is of rawhide and turned up all around.   When the toe piece is
sewed in position the part of the upper marked *c* and *d* is sewed around the
heel, *c* joining that part of the toe piece near the centre on the outer side of

the foot and *d* joining on the opposite side, the lacing point leading across
the instep, the edge of which from *d* to *e* is sewed to
the edge of the toe piece, the end of the point reaching
to a button below the ankle. The sewing of the
upper to the sole is from the outside.

When of rawhide, the soles of all moccasins conform to the shape of the foot rather than to conven-
tion. The Comanche, however, use a truly conventional sole (Fig. 99). The line along the inner side
of the sole, excepting the curves at the heel and toe,
is straight, following the shape of the foot around the
toes, to a point rather back of the centre of the tread,
thence tapering back to the heel with another straight
line. The soft leather of the upper lends itself to the
shape of the stiff sole and a moccasin of angular
appearance is the result.

Fig. 99.   The Comanche
Sole.

One common form of lacing or draw string prevails, that of passing a thong through slits in the
sides of the upper, and around the heel (Fig. 100). The lace is tied over
the instep in the case of low moccasins and where an
extension or ankle flap has been added, a thong of
sufficient length to wind around the leg above the ankle
is used. Where this form of lacing is not employed,
a short thong is sewed to the edge of the flap where
the end of the lace would come out if it had been
threaded around in the usual way. The variations
in lacing and in the extensions that have been observed
in the area, seem to have a general distribution.
Some tribes, especially the Blackfoot, use a kind of
rudimentary flap on the extensions suggesting the pendant ones so characteristic of the Iroquois and other eastern tribes.[1]

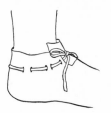

Fig. 100.   The Lace.

The only attempt at a comparative study of moccasin patterns coming
to our notice, is a recent article by H. Ling Roth.[2] This writer described
four patterns corresponding to our Nos. 3, 4, 8, and 12. It may be noted
that he finds our pattern No. 12 among the Kickapoo, an observation we
have not been able to verify for lack of authentic material. In our study
we have so far given attention to these general patterns only, passing all
that may be considered ornamental or secondary for future discussion.

A large number (271) of moccasins in the Museum's collection were

---

[1] Mr. Orchard's contribution ends here.
[2] Roth, 47.

classified according to the preceding patterns and their relative distributions given in the table. It is clear that moccasins of the two piece type prevail almost exclusively in the southwest of interior North America and those of one piece in the woodlands of the east and north. So far as our table goes, in the Missouri-Saskatchewan area the Blackfoot and the Sarcee show the strongest inclination to use the one piece type. As previously stated, the Blackfoot winter moccasin was of the one piece type which seems also to have been the case among the Gros Ventre and many divisions of the Dakota. While our data is not complete, it suggests the Missouri-Saskatchewan area as the border land between tribes using the two types of moccasins, the one well adapted to winter use, the other to summer wear. The inference is, that the soled type came in from the southwest, perhaps an adaptation of the sandal idea. The Blackfoot claim to have traditional knowledge that the soled type is the later form. In any event, they show both northern and southern characteristics.

THE RELATIVE DISTRIBUTION OF MOCCASIN PATTERNS.

Patterns	1	2	3	4	5	6	7	8	9	10	11	12	13	14	15	16	17	18	Totals
Naskapi											1								1
Montagnais											1								1
Iroquois							6												6
Shawnee							1												1
Ojibway											5								5
Cree								5			10								15
Mackenzie											11								11
Thompson								2		1	1								4
Nez Perce	1							1											2
Sarcee	2		16		1			4											23
Assiniboine	13							1			1								15
Crow	13																		13
Blackfoot	6		7					3											16
Gros Ventre	5		4					1											10
Bannock	2																		2
Dakota (Teton)	39	1	3								2		1						46
Mandan	2																		2
Cheyenne	2																		2
Arapaho	17		4										3						24
Shoshone	20		2		1		1												24
Ute	20			5									2						27
Comanche	1		2										6						9
Apache						2										3			5
Hopi														2	1			1	4
Zuni																	1		1
Ft. Leavenworth										1	1								2

As to hair dressing for men, three features may be taken for comparison: the fore lock, the lengthened tresses, and hair painting. The trailing back ornament of quill-covered strips of rawhide and later a beaded ornament, general among the Assiniboine, Gros Ventre, Dakota and the village Indians seems not to have been adopted by the Blackfoot. Taking the drawings by Bodmer and Catlin as probably correct, we find the fore lock among the following: Assiniboine, Yankton (Dakota), Hidatsa, Mandan, Arikara, Kootenai, Nez Perce and Kiowa, suggesting a wide range of distribution. Lengthening the hair by sections held on by gum has been mentioned among the Mandan, Arikara, Hidatsa, Gros Ventre, Assiniboine, Dakota, Arapaho, Kiowa, Comanche, Cheyenne and Nez Perce.[1] It is probable, however, that some of these observers have mistaken the detached headdress used by the Blackfoot and of which there is a specimen in the Nez Perce collection. Painting the hair was usual among the village Indians, Henry stating that "they daub it afresh every morning" with "red earth." [2] The Cree used paint sparingly and the Assiniboine regularly.[3] Though information on this point is not definite, it seems that the disinclination of the Blackfoot to paint their hair differentiates them somewhat from the tribes to whom they in other respects bear great resemblance.

Something like the knot used by some Blackfoot men seems to have been used by the Cree and Assiniboine; though from the description, the resemblance of the latter to eastern Eskimo styles is suggested.[3]

In conclusion, it may be well to note that the Missouri-Saskatchewan area may be characterized by men's hair being worn in natural and even artificial lengths while among the Quapaw, Otto, Osage, Pawnee, Kickapoo, Sauk and Fox and many eastern tribes, the hair on the sides of the head was cut close or shaved leaving ridges or tufts on the top.[4] Some Tetons informed the writer, that there was a saying among their old people to the effect that such was one time common among them, though so far no historical support to such a belief has come to our knowledge. We may say then, that the love of long, heavy tresses was greatly accentuated among the tribes of the Missouri-Saskatchewan area and while the Blackfoot may not have entered into this as keenly as some others, they nevertheless manifest it as a cultural trait.

The hair of the women throughout the area was usually worn in the two-braid fashion with the medium part from the forehead to the neck. In

---

[1] James 1, 161; 3, 46; Maximilian, 259; Henry and Thompson, 342, 347; Clark, 134.
[2] Henry and Thompson, 325.
[3] Henry and Thompson, 515, 517.
[4] Maximilian, 159.

Henry's time, however, the Cree women seem to have worn a large knot behind each ear.[1]

As to the breech cloth being a recent acquisition of the Blackfoot, Henry may be correct. Harmon gives one the impression that the Carriers, in his day, seldom used them, if at all.[2] Some early accounts of the interior Salish give a similar impression. The men occupying these areas seem to have worn long shirts and leggings in contrast to those in our area, rendering the use of a breech cloth unnecessary. The Crow are believed to have adopted it in modern times and, while in Maximilian's time, it was worn by the Mandan, La Vérendrye, their first observer, found it entirely wanting.[3] The Cree[4] used the regular form described for the Blackfoot, which seems to have been general throughout the area, at least since the opening of the historical period. The suggestion is, however, that the breech cloth was introduced to the area by traders.

Since robes were simply the skins of buffalo, their shape was fixed. The decorations differed somewhat among the different tribes, but the band with three or more disks, or rosettes, seems to have been in general use throughout the entire area. In Maximilian's day, the village Indians were taking to the wide bands like the Blackfoot, having previously used narrow ones. It appears from the collections we have examined that the very wide bands were in recent years confined to the Blackfoot and their immediate neighbors.

---

[1] Henry and Thompson, 515

[2] Harmon, 245.

[3] Recent information secured by G. L. Wilson makes it reasonably certain that the breech-cloth was introduced among the village Indians after their first contact with traders.

[4] Henry and Thompson, 515, 517.

Weapons and Warfare.

Henry, who had traded long with many tribes to the eastward, states over and over again that war was the chief activity of the Blackfoot. In one part of his journal, we find the following:—

"War seems to be the Piegan's sole delight; their discourse always turns upon that subject; one war-party no sooner arrives than another sets off. Horses are the principal plunder to be obtained from these enemies on the W. Formerly the Flat Heads and other tribes became an easy prey, and were either killed or driven away like sheep, but within a few years they have acquired firearms and become formidable. The severe defeat the Piegans sustained last summer did not discourage them from renewed enterprises of the same nature. They are always the aggressors; there never has an instance been known of a native coming to war from the W. side of the mountains. The Crows are the only nation that sometimes venture northward in search of the slaves. The Snakes are a miserable, defenseless nation, who never venture abroad. The Piegans call them old women, whom they can kill with sticks and stones. They take great delight in relating their adventures in war, and are so vivid in rehearsing every detail of the fray that they seem to be fighting the battle over again. A Piegan takes as much pleasure in the particulars of the excursion in which he is engaged as a Saulteur does in relating a grand drinking match—how many nights they were drunk and how many kegs of liquor they consumed." [1]

In other parts of his journal, he expresses similar estimates of the Blood and other divisions so that what he assigns to the Piegan, was to his mind in no way peculiar to them alone. While Henry was always a severe critic of the Indian, his comparisons give the impression that he found a contrast in this respect between the Blackfoot on the one hand and the Cree and Ojibway on the other. This seems to imply that the Blackfoot attitude toward war was similar to that of their southern neighbors.

We have found it impossible to secure information as to the mode of warfare before the introduction of horses and firearms. Each of these innovations in turn, must have made a great change, since the most probable tendency would be for the Blackfoot to imitate the methods of those introducing the respective equipments. Until within thirty years, the firearms traded these Indians were of no great efficiency and their skill with them was held in some contempt by early observers. Some of these observers mention the carrying of what appeared to be an extra ram rod for their muzzle loaders, but according to our informants, this was used as a support, or rest, when firing.

---

[1] Henry and Thompson, 726.

As elsewhere, the stealing of horses was almost a synonym for war, raids being made without reserve upon all their neighbors, except at such times as a truce might be established. There were even occasions on which men from one division raided the horses of another, but such was not approved by the large majority in all divisions. The manner of conducting such raids belongs, however, to another part of our research. When out for plunder, the feeling was that, if horses could be secured and if attacked, their owners frightened off without loss to either side, the affair was a success, for killing the enemy was not quite up to the standard. However, expeditions for scalps and for revenge were sometimes made and with a different attitude. When fighting mounted they, like other tribes, protected their bodies by hanging on the sides of the horses. The charge was a rush in a compact body, scattering along the front of the enemy as they passed, in order to deliver their fire.

Nothing in the way of fortifications was used except such improvised affairs as the occasion demanded. When a party was hard pressed by superior numbers, it took refuge in a natural or hastily constructed pit. Once so intrenched with a liberal supply of ammunition, a large number of opponents were easily beaten off. For protection against night attacks, war parties made use of "war lodges." These were made by setting up heavy poles forming a conical hut, the door of which was protected by a curved covered way. Such a structure not only concealed the fire, but made defence against a night attack easy. Sometimes a rectangular structure was made, the walls converging to the apex. All of these forms were used by other tribes as well. They stood along war trails and were kept in repair from year to year.

Scalping was common, though the counting of coup and the capture of weapons seems to have been of greater significance. So far as our information goes, there was less interest in preserving scalps than among many other tribes, the usual practice being to throw them away after the women's dance.

Bows, Arrows, and Quivers. The bow has been out of use so long, that good, practical specimens are scarcely to be found and accurate knowledge concerning them difficult to secure. The collection contains few bows, only one of which can be considered as designed for use as a weapon, the others being intended for gaming by youths and boys. This specimen was collected in 1870. It is sinew-backed and now somewhat warped as shown in Fig. 101. The length in its present condition is 105 cm. The grip is wrapped with a narrow thong, apparently of buffalo hide. The ends for a distance of 10 cm. are encased in a membrane of some sort, probably an intestine. The sinew back is painted green and the remainder of the surface red. The string is of sinew. When in good condition, and strung, this bow was evi-

dently of the double curve-type.   A similar bow made by a Blood, examined
by the writer had such a curve and was in other respects similar to the
specimen just described.[1]   The game bows are simple wooden affairs, apparently cut from slender stems of the birch.   Their lengths are 116, 110 and

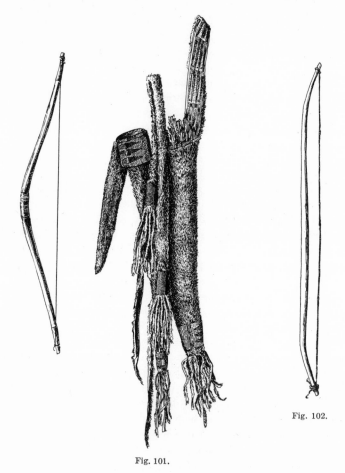

Fig. 102.

Fig. 101.

Fig. 101.   A Bow and Quiver.   Length of *a*, 107 cm., *b*, 84 cm.
Fig. 102 (50–5732).   A Bow.   Length, 120 cm.

97 cm.   The shapes are those of Fig. 102, varying in the amount of curvature.
It will be observed that none of these are straight but show a reverse curve
at the belly.

[1] See Catlin, 1, Plate 18, for a drawing of a similar bow.

The strings to the bows are of sinew. At one end a noose slips over notches when the bow is strung while at the other the string is tied in similar notches with the extra length wound around the bow. Thus these bows are doubled nocked. Ash was the favorite bow wood.

Arrows were usually made of service berry wood though sometimes of willow. The shaft was of a single piece and feathered. The quiver accompanying the bow in Fig. 101 contains thirteen arrows with iron points. The shafts vary in length from 55 to 58 cm. The feathers are three in number, about 18 cm. in length and arranged at approximately equal distances around the shaft. Although these feathers are not always exactly parallel to the shaft, it has evidently been the intention of the maker to have them so. The feathers seem to be from the wing of a hawk, split through the quill and trimmed to a width of about 1 cm. at the top, tapering away on the quill. The ends of the quills are bound to the shaft by many turns of sinew or narrow bands of some membrane. The points are about 7 cm. long and 2 cm. wide at the base, inserted in a notch about 1 cm. deep and bound with sinew or membrane. The feathers have been dyed; on nine of the arrows they are red, on four they are yellow. Near the notched end is the usual band of color. On the arrows with red feathers, this consists of a band of blue about 5 cm. in width, extending around the shaft with a narrow border of red above and below. The other arrows bear an unbordered band of green about the same width. These four seem to differ from the others also in that the shafts have three to four shallow longitudinal grooves. They may have been made by a different person. The notches are V-shaped and the nocks bulbous. At the bases of the quills to the feathers, are bound small bits of plume, or soft feathers.

The collection contains seven arrows with bone points made recently by an old man as models. The shafts appear to be of willow and are heavy, being 1 cm. in thickness, or about twice that of the preceding. Their total length varies from 65 to 67 cm. The feathers are 20 cm. in length and arranged as in the preceding. The markings are different being a band of dark red below the notch, about 9 cm. wide, bordered on the lower edge by blue about 1 cm. in width and separated from the red by a border of equal width without color. The shafts are grooved with two to three waving irregular lines. The arrows for the game sets are somewhat longer than those just described. According to Morse, the Blackfoot used the tertiary release.[1]

While there are traditions of stone headed arrows, the claim most frequently made is that, preceding the introduction of iron, points of bone

---

[1] Morse, 3–52.

and of deer horn were used. According to some informants some were made from buffalo horns, this material being easily worked when softened by heating. Grinnell writes that metal points "were of two kinds — barbed slender points for war, and barbless for hunting." [1] This agrees with Catlin's sketches.[2]

Some writers have made the statement that arrow-heads were either parallel or at right angles to the plane of the notch — according to use. For killing buffalo, they were vertical, for men horizontal, so that they might pass more easily between the ribs.[3] No one among the present Blackfoot seemed to have heard of such a distinction. The heads of arrows in the collection seem to be chiefly horizontal, but many are vertical and others oblique. On the whole, it appears that no great effort was made to set them at any exact angle. The only difference reported for war arrows was a disposition to bind the heads loosely, so that they would remain in the wound, after the shaft was withdrawn.

With the bow (Fig. 101) is a combined quiver and bow-case made of otter skin. The quiver is almost as long as the case and joined to it with a thong by a peculiar wrapping stitch over a stick which keeps the two from collapse. Around the top and bottom of each is a broad beaded strip of elk hide. At the bottoms are fringes of strips of otter skin. From the top of the quiver, hangs a long pointed appendage of otter skin, backed by a piece of beaded elk skin of similar shape. From the top of the bow case hangs a piece of otter skin of similar shape. The carrying strap is of otter skin, fastened to the stick, over which the thong joining the two is wrapped. At the two points where attached, are two large tassels of otter skin, bound by a band of beaded elk skin. At the top of the quiver is a peculiar upright object about 15 cm. high made by wrapping a strip of rawhide around a piece of brass wire. According to our information, this was always placed in quivers, but knowledge of its significance has been lost. The size is that of an ordinary lead pencil. The surface is beaded and to the top are tied two small strips of otter skin. This is probably a charm. Maximilian says of the Blackfoot:— "For their quivers they prefer the skin of a cougouar, for which they give a horse. The tail hangs down from the quiver, is trimmed with red cloth on the inner side, embroidered with white beads, and ornamented at the end or elsewhere, with strips of skin, like tassels." [4] Catlin also describes bows and quivers and says that the skins of otters were used for quivers.[5] Maximilian's atlas contains sketches of Blackfoot Indians bearing

[1] Grinnell, (a), 200.
[2] Catlin, 1, Plate 18.
[3] Mason, (d), 661.
[4] Maximilian, 257.
[5] Catlin, 1, 32.

quivers to which are attached long flaps bearing designs, chiefly of the rosette type. This would indicate the general use of such flaps at that time. A similar ornament also appears on a Snake Indian quiver described by Mason.[1]

We are indebted to Professor O. T. Mason for an extensive comparative study of North American Indian bows.[2] He regards the self-bow, or the simple wooden bow, as characteristic of the Mississippi basin and the Atlantic slope, while west of the Rocky Mountains in the United States and British Columbia, the sinew-lined, or sinew-backed bow prevails. In this westward area he claims two types of sinew-backed bows, a broad, flat, short type and a long slender narrow type. The latter was distributed among the Shoshonean tribes, Canadian Athapascan, Apache, Navajo and Pueblo tribes further south. To quote directly:— " The Athapascan sinew veneered bow is found strictly west of the Rockies, the slender variety in the Basin and British Columbia, the flat variety on the Pacific Slope. The Navajo also have adopted this type of sinew-lined bow." [3] If this were strictly true, the sinew-backed bow should be denied the Blackfoot, whereas we have just described specimens of the long, narrow, slender type. In the Museum collection we find similar bows among the Cheyenne and the Arapaho and according to Kroeber, they were used by the Gros Ventre.[4] All of these tribes, however, lived on the eastern border of the sinew-backed bow area. On the other hand, as stated by Mason, bows of the compound type reinforced with sinew, were known to the Indians of the Upper Missouri. These bows were made of horn and have been described by Bradbury [5] and Clark.[6] The Museum's collections contain a Nez Perce bow made of sheep horn. This bow is sinew-backed. The descriptions of horn bows from the Upper Missouri just cited do not make it clear that they are sinew-backed, yet such must have been the case. We may assume, then, that the sinew-backed bows, of whatever type, found among the tribes east of the Rocky Mountains are intrusive. This assumption is further supported by the fact that among the Plains tribes where sinew-backed bows were in use, the statements of travelers imply them to have been exceptional rather than general, the simple wooden bow being the prevailing type.

In the Museum collections, the Blackfoot and Northern Cheyenne sinew-backed bows are most like those of the Nez Perce, while those accredited to the Arapaho and Ute are much shorter and of a different curve. That

[1] Mason (d), Plate 87.
[2] Mason (d), 631–680; Plates 37–94.
[3] Mason, (d), 640.
[4] Kroeber, (a), 151.
[5] Early Western Travels, 5, 172.
[6] Clark, 78.

the Blackfoot acquired this type of bow from the west is made more probable by the following from Henry's journal:—

"The bows used by the natives W. of the mountains are neatly made, and of three kinds — the horn, the red cedar, and the plain wooden bow. The horn bow is made of a slip of ram's horn. The outside is left undressed, but overlaid with several successive layers of sinew glued to the thickness of one-third of an inch, and then covered with rattlesnake skin. The inside is smoothly polished, and displays the several ridges of the horn. These neat bows are about three feet long, and throw an arrow an amazing distance. The red cedar bow is made of a slip of that wood, overlaid with sinew and glue like the horn bow, and also well polished inside; it is nearly four feet long, and throws an arrow a great distance. The plain wooden bow is of cedar, willow, or ash; the outside is untouched, except that the bark is removed. It is well smoothed, but not so much esteemed by the natives as either kind of sinew bows. These people make the handsomest bows I have ever seen — always preferred by other Indians. I have known a Piegan to give a gun or horse for one of those made of sinew." [1]

Many years later, Maximilian observes that the Blackfoot are less skillful in the manufacture of weapons than the Crows, Hidatsa and Mandans and that "they do not themselves make bows of the horn of the elk, or of the mountain sheep, which are consequently not common among them." [2]

The simple wooden bows of the Missouri-Saskatchewan area show some tribal differences. As previously noted, those we have collected from the Blackfoot show a slight double curve. This is quite pronounced in the Dakota bows we have examined. On the other hand, those we have seen from the Sarcee, Comanche and Shoshone were of the single curve type. This suggests a general uniformity in the Missouri-Saskatchewan area. Professor Mason regards the single lower nock as universal among Plains tribes, but in the Museum collection of Dakota bows, we find both the single and double nock. The same appears to be true of bows credited to the Comanche and Shoshone. So far as our observation goes, all the sinew-backed bows are double nocked though in a manner different from simple wooden bows. The Sarcee bows we have seen are double nocked like those of the Blackfoot. Thus, the two methods of nocking appear about equally distributed in the area.

The arrows used in the Missouri-Saskatchewan area were shorter than those west of the Rocky Mountains and probably shorter than those of the eastern woodland Indians. They are all three-feathered. According to the Museum collection, Blackfoot arrows are about the same average length (65 cm.) as those of the Sarcee, Dakota and Cheyenne. Those of the

---

[1] Henry and Thompson, 713–714.

[2] Maximilian, 257. For information as to methods of manufacture, comparative qualities and modes of handling sinew-backed bows see Clark, 77; Henry and Thompson, 714.

Shoshone are somewhat longer and those of the Comanche shorter. The color bands near the nock show considerable variation among the different tribes. The Blackfoot varies from two to three; the Cheyenne, none to one; the Dakota, one to three; the Shoshone uniformly two; the Comanche and Sarcee many bands of color.

The claim is sometimes made that these color bands are ownership marks; but we have failed to find any evidence that such was the case. It is true that each man recognized his own arrows, but so far as we know, this was by the same means by which we identify our own writing; i. e., not by a definite system of marks but by general individuality. We have observed such differences between the contents of quivers from the same tribe and it is a matter of general experience that hand-workers everywhere have no difficulty in recognizing their products regardless of specific marks.

There are some important differences in the length of the feathering. For the arrows measured, they ranged as follows:

	Cm.
Blackfoot	18–20
Sarcee	15–16
Cheyenne	14–23
Dakota	16–19
Shoshone	11–13
Comanche	10–12

The shafts of the Dakota arrows we have seen are grooved as are also those of the Cheyenne. Those of the Shoshone and Comanche are not grooved. However, according to Mason, the Apache, Comanche, Ute, Shoshone and also the Pawnee used grooved arrows. The practice seems not to have been universal in any tribe.

While this discussion of arrows has not shown anything very characteristic for the Blackfoot as members of the Missouri-Saskatchewan group, it indicates a general uniformity in this group as opposed to southern and western tribes.

The combined bow case and quiver is frequently met with among the Missouri-Saskatchewan tribes. The two are joined together and usually stiffened by a stick. The ends of the carrying strap usually hang down and are fringed. The Museum collection contains specimens of this type from the Blackfoot, Cheyenne, Dakota, Sarcee, Comanche and Shoshone. Among those for the Cheyenne and the Comanche we find examples of the long triangular flaps noted for the Blackfoot. The Shoshone collection contains two quivers in which the bow is carried with the arrows. The specific type of bow case and quiver shown in Fig. 101 has been found among the southern Cheyenne, Kiowa, Dakota, Northern Shoshone, Nez Perce,

Ute, Crow, and Sarcee. Maximilian credits the Mandan, Hidatsa and Crow with the long quiver flap, lined with red cloth and decorated with rosettes.[1] The closest parallels, however, are found among tribes immediately to the east, south and west of the Blackfoot. Nez Perce quivers figured by Mason (Plates 78 and 90) are strikingly like that of Fig. 101. In one case the designs on the long flaps are almost identical. Also a Snake Indian quiver bearing similar flap ornaments has been described by Mason.[2]

Returning to our previous statements implying that the Blackfoot looked westward for their bows, it may be added that we find no evidences of such intrusion with respect to arrows. This exception, however, seems to support our conclusions. All the evidence indicates that the older type of Blackfoot bow and arrow was that of the ethnographical area in which they resided and that this bow was partially displaced by importations of compound and sinew-backed types, while the importation of arrows was obviously impracticable. On the other hand, the Blackfoot type of quiver was found immediately east, south and west of their habitat.

Lances. Though Maximilian[3] saw few lances among the Blackfoot, according to our information they were at one time in general use. This direct testimony is supported by the fact that lances formed a conspicuous part of the regalia for societies composed of warriors. All the specimens we have seen, however, are ceremonial rather than practical; hence, their description will be postponed. The use of a combined bow and spear; i. e., a bow with a lance head on one end, seems to have been unknown though common in the Missouri valley and some parts of the interior of British Columbia.

Shields. The circular buffalo hide shield was in general use. Those in our collection are about 49 cm. in diameter. The skin is very hard, and about 2 cm. in thickness. One specimen is about 2 cm. thick but apparently two ply. They are not flat, but dished to a depth of about 8 cm. The painted and other decorations are usually placed directly upon the shield and not upon a cover as is done by the Crow, Dakota, and some other tribes. However, one specimen in our collection bears the design upon a cover. Around the circumference of the shield is a strip of red cloth about 9 cm. in width to which are hung eagle feathers varying in number, according to our observations, from 19 to 28. The decorations are always upon the dished, or flesh side of the skin. While the Dakota often used horse hide for the shield, the Blackfoot seem to have used buffalo hide exclusively.

The true cover, not to be confused with the inner facing just mentioned,

---

[1] Maximilian, 389.
[2] Mason, (d), Plate 87.
[3] Maximilian, 258.

is of soft buckskin fitted with a draw string of the same material. Such covers are to protect the designs and feathers, the latter being turned back into the dished hollow before the cover is put in place.[1] As a rule, no decorations occur on such covers but two covers coming to our notice had simple decorations. One had a small circle at the centre, another a transverse buckskin fringe. The decorations upon Blackfoot shields together with their ceremonial functions will be discussed in a future paper. The designs are usually in black, red and green.[2]

A general comparison of the shields available indicates that those of the Blackfoot and Cheyenne are approximately 49 cm. in diameter, those of the Crow a little larger, while those of the Dakota range near 43 cm. Some Comanche shields seen by the writer were nearly 60 cm. in diameter. According to Lewis and Clark those made by the Northern Shoshone were about 75 cm. in diameter.[3] Though the number of specimens herein considered is not large, the result suggests tribal standards as to size.

When a shield was to be made, a buffalo bull was skinned by cutting down the back. A large piece from the breast was taken, laid on the ground, hair side up and soaked with boiling water which loosened the hair and caused the shrinkage. Finally, the skin was turned over while wet and shaped over a small heap of earth and weighted down for drying. It was this heap of earth that gave the peculiar dish observed in these shields. The hair was removed with a stone, not with a scraper (p. 66). The last step in the process was to trim the edges to a circle previously marked out by a stick.[4]

Armor. Wooden armor seems to have been unknown but there are traditions implying that buckskin shirts of two or more thicknesses were worn as protection against stone and bone points. This suggests borrowed ideas from tribes west of the mountains.

Clubs. The well known stone-headed war club was in use, though simple short cudgels of wood were very common. Three types of stone-headed clubs seem to have been known; the pointed club, the club with a ball, and the ax-shaped club. The club with a ball is shown in Fig. 103 and bears a close resemblance to some clubs seen in collections from the Nez Perce though the type also occurs among the Dakota. In the specimen figured, a rounded stone is sewed up in a skin cover, an extension of which forms the sheath for a wooden handle. No specimen of the ax type came

---

[1] One informant gave the following suggestive information:— Shields were dish-shaped and could be sprung in or out. When not in use, they were sprung in and covered with the buckskin cover. The standard size for a shield was that the pendant feathers should just reach the centre when turned inward.

[2] Maximilian, 258.

[3] Lewis and Clark, 3, 19.

[4] For a good account of the Northern Shoshone method see Lewis and Clark, 3, 20.

to our notice, but according to descriptions, it is similar to the specimen figured by Maximilian.[1]   There are traditions that this was the prevailing

Fig. 103 (50–5422).   A War Club.   Length, 80 cm.

type; also it was used in killing buffalo when wounded in the pound.   The double pointed stone club head of the Dakota seems not to have been in use.

---

[1] Maximilian, 179.

GENERAL DISCUSSION.

As a matter of convenience we offer at the outset of this discussion a brief summary of the results attained in the comparative sections of the preceding paper. In order to minimize the chances for misunderstandings let us make, in the first place, a mere statement of fact. We found no direct evidence that the Blackfoot had ever occupied any other territory than their range in the time of Henry (1808), except in so far as remote linguistic relationship may be considered such evidence. Certain Blackfoot processes and choices in berry foods bear resemblance to Dene traits, while the methods of handling camas are identical with those of the Nez Perce and neighboring tribes. In the choice of other foods the Blackfoot are scarcely to be distinguished from the other tribes of the area, nor as to processes except that their cooking is more suggestive of the interior plateaus than otherwise. They, like their immediate neighbors, did not cultivate corn. In manufactures and the arts they show striking uniformity with the other buffalo hunting tribes even in many minor details of technique, though on the other hand they show slight inclinations toward Western Cree and Dene types in contrast to the almost entire absence of such among their immediate neighbors. In all that pertains to shelter and to transportation by horse or dog they show little individuality. In costume the true Blackfoot characteristics were to be found in a few minor details of decoration and not in general pattern and scheme. Perhaps this may be clearer if presented in a statistical fashion. Taking as their near neighbors the Plains Cree, Assiniboine, Sarcee, Gros Ventre, Crow, Nez Perce and Hidatsa we find the following traits quite similar in all essential details among the great majority, the very few positive exceptions having been noted in the text: — methods of cooking, buffalo pounds, skin dressing, travois, cradles, quivers and sinew backed bows, war lodges, shirts for men, black striped leggings, blanket bands, weasel skin ornaments, wide belts for women, caps for men and fringed bags. It is not necessary to our purpose to make this list complete. It is plain that most of these parallels to Blackfoot traits are found on the east and south. There are, for example, relatively few traits closely analogous to those of the interior Salish, the western and eastern Athapascan. While there are some striking similarities between the Blackfoot and Nez Perce, the latter seem to show greater relation to the Hidatsa and Crow. On this point more information is needed. In a previous publication we have noted some mythological parallels between the Blackfoot and the

Crow. Thus we have the suggestion that the Hidatsa and Crow have influenced the Blackfoot on one hand and the Nez Perce on the other. However, this must remain tentative until further data are available.

Bearing in mind that the traits enumerated above are also in common peculiar to the immediate neighbors of the Blackfoot as a group of Plains people, we may turn to the enumeration of Blackfoot traits widely distributed among the tribes of the Missouri basin and the Shoshone area. Among these we find great uniformity in: — antelope drives, eagle traps, paunch vessels, horn spoons, skin dressing tools, mauls, travois, tipis, riding gear, shields, men's ornamented shirts, legging bands, soled moccasins, buffalo robes, long hair for men, woman's dress and leggings, spliced hair for men, parfleche and square bags, globular skin rattles and flageolettes.

Of traits widely distributed among these tribes but practically foreign to the Blackfoot we have noted the strike-a-light pouch, elaborate body painting, the soft striped bag (p. 74), the flat hanging hair ornament. The somewhat trifling character and small number of these as opposed to the tipi, riding-gear, etc., all of which appear in the culture of the Blackfoot serve to emphasize the almost overwhelming similarity of material traits throughout the Missouri-Saskatchewan area in which this tribe resides. Facing about to enumerate the traits entirely peculiar to the Blackfoot we seek almost in vain. A few objects such as bags made of deer's feet, their type of pipe bag and men's toilet bags while rare in the Plains are common northward. Thus eliminating the traits of material culture common to other tribes we have left almost nothing that the Blackfoot can call their own.

Having now made at least a sample invoice of the data observable, we may give some space to a discussion of the problems and interpretations therein suggested. In the first place, confining ourselves to the limits of the data presented, it may be asked in how far we are justified in speaking of a Blackfoot material culture at all. About the only defence we can make for our title is that we have a people speaking one language, a definite obvious social bond, and that we have a right to determine what their habits are regardless. Now, in the discussion of this Blackfoot material culture we have, as it were, uncovered a larger whole of which it is in the main an integral part. Taking our stand with the Blackfoot and turning our eyes to the buffalo country, or to the geographical area of which their lands are a part, we see first a very slight diminution of traits among immediate tribes and a few glimpses of strange ways, then as we look beyond increasing and ever greater divergence until little is familiar. The region in which the uniformity is decidedly to the fore is the combined drainage of the Missouri and the Saskatchewan — for convenience, the Missouri-Saskatchewan culture area. Thus, for those who take stock in precise definition, it may be admitted that, in even a specific sense, we should say that the Blackfoot manifest the material culture of the Missouri-Saskatchewan area and speak of a Blackfoot culture only in the case of those few minor details in which they show their individuality.   On the other hand, we must not overlook the existence of variation among the individuals composing the various divisions of the Blackfoot.   It must not be assumed that the detailed statements in the preceding hold absolutely for all individuals, for in the field we have seen from time to time touches of individual initiative and originality in their turn copied by others.   The naïve assumption is often made, even by those who should know better, that custom is absolute in the culture of American races, whereas those cultures we have actually experienced not only show a considerable range in variability, but also seem to be subject to frequent changes and transitions.   This applies even to well developed methods of procedure; as for example, the Blackfoot method of setting up a tipi from which a few women so far departed as to use a method found among other tribes.   While in theory, at least, some of these variations and departures from prevailing customs we have observed are destined to become in turn prevalent, we have for obvious reasons presented in this paper chiefly those that were found to prevail at least among a considerable fraction of the people.   As this is a relative criterion there are chances for obser- vatival errors on the part of every field-worker that should not be entirely ignored.   Further, if we take the view that the only thing worth while in anthropology is to offer data as to how a definite linguistic unit manages to work out a culture, the ignoring of these individual variations may lead to abortive results in that we reject the very phenomena in which at least a part of the process is underway.   However, since anthropology now seems to concern itself with cultures rather than with the individuals who practise them, it may be best to think of the case as the culture found in function among people speaking the Blackfoot language.   Hence, we choose to define our theoretical problem from this point of view, not forgetting that here culture is but a generalized statement of many variable activities in the manifestation of which the individuals concerned are not by any means so stereotyped as some writers would have us believe.

To return to the Blackfoot, the plain question that arises with all and refuses to down is, how came these people by this culture?   If the preceding pages had described customs wholly unique, we could all agree that, aside from some troublesome presuppositions of linguistic theories, there were no probable reasons why they did not themselves create this culture.   Since directly the opposite tendency is observable the matter is not so simple. Obviously several alternatives in whole or in part may be proposed: the whole culture may have originated with the Blackfoot and have been passed on to other tribes; it may have originated contemporaneously but independently among several or all the different tribes; the Blackfoot may have developed some traits, other tribes still others, a gradual selection having taken place until the whole area came to the same level. Two greatly overworked theories have been requisitioned by their respective partisans to account for similarities of culture: viz., the independent development theory and the diffusion theory. Those who hold to the former may say that the general uniformity of economic conditions and the similarity of materials throughout the area would in time bring all to adopt independently the same material culture. Now, it may be conceded that this will account for some things; the use of buffalo robes, for example. Again, if there were no buffalo to hunt except within two widely separated areas, the case would be clear; but neither the general distribution of buffalo nor their uniform habits will make it certain that a number of tribes would each develop a drive on the same detailed plan. Even were this true, how could we account for the wearing of artificially lengthened hair, particular cut of dress and bag within the same area without doing violence to all experience with probabilities? As we have just remarked, we have a culture spread over the area in which the Blackfoot are incidentally found among other tribes, a point of view that renders serious consideration of the independent theory out of question for this particular case. Turning to the theory of diffusion, we find our feet nearer solid ground for we have found that in keeping with their position on the frontier of the area the Blackfoot show some traits similar to those beyond the borders and that within the area itself the Blackfoot and their immediate neighbors can be differentiated somewhat from the others. Without offering many more even weightier reasons, we may accept the theory of diffusion as the most satisfactory explanation so far presented.

We come now to the specific problem of Blackfoot culture which narrows down to a question of cultural priority in whole or in part. Here we are forced to confess an almost hopeless task for the dominant anthropological method assumes to be historical, while here historical data seem to fail us. We can only infer that the Blackfoot as an ethnic unit were not always inhabitants of the area on the basis of linguistic relationship which is far from final. In defining the distribution of cultural traits as we have done we can only at best make a few doubtful inferences as to the part the Blackfoot took in their diffusion. It may be possible to determine lines of affiliation and tribal intercourse at the opening of the historic period and correlate them with the distribution of cultural details.[1] For example, there was at one time, some intermarriage between the Blackfoot and Sarcee, Gros

---

[1] Wissler, (d).

Ventre, Cree and Flathead; and captive women of the Shoshone, Crow, Assiniboine and in short of all tribes with whom they were at war, were brought home and retained. Thus in peace as well as war there must have been many opportunities for becoming acquainted with the cultural traits of others. There is every reason to believe that some native trade existed long before the advent of the fur dealer and that along these lost trails passed and repassed many tribal arts. Such a method applied to the area at large promises results of importance, but the difficulty in our present narrow problem is that even at the opening of the historic period the Blackfoot stand out as a powerful nucleus. Thus while early traders report many persons among the neighboring tribes who had learned Blackfoot, they found the Blackfoot unable to speak foreign languages. This with other data of like tenor implies that, long before the opening of the historic period, these people were dominant in their area and its environs and on this assumption must have played some part in the formation of the culture of the Missouri-Saskatchewan area. Further, we may then assume that such traits as are dominant among them and minor among their neighbors were original, but it is well to bear in mind that we are piling up assumption on assumption. However, if we accept the Grinnell theory that the Blackfoot are but recent arrivals from the forests, then part of our problem is solved — they borrowed the whole thing, lost every vestige of their own material culture and originated nothing.

When, however, we turn to the area as a whole and consider the cultures on its borders, the case is not quite so hopeless. Take for example what meagre data we gathered on the tipi. The mere matter of pole arrangement arrays the Blackfoot, Crow, Hidatsa, Sarcee and Comanche as opposing the Dakota, Assiniboine, Cheyenne, Arapaho and Gros Ventre; while students of Indian history have claimed early tribal contacts that are in the main consistent with this grouping. However, a careful examination of all tipis, an ultimate grouping for all tipi users and a re-valuation of historical data, are sufficiently promising to warrant further researches. Again, the distribution of analogous forms of tipi-like structures offers a basis for fairly satisfactory inferences as to the centres of distribution for the specific features of this type of shelter. In this as in all other tracings of resemblance in culture we must avoid the general and the essential. Thus an experiment will make it clear that to put up a tipi the natural course will be to tie three or four poles, but that beyond that there are many ways of accomplishing the desired practical result without the uniformity in the orders of placing the poles we have observed. In all cases it is full detailed data we need. The present tendency among many field-workers is to be satisfied with the very general and give us such bare statements as they use tipis and first set up three poles, statements good as far as they go but as we have seen quite deficient in the solution of cultural problems.   Details, trivial in themselves, are likely to contribute more to the result than a wealth of repeated general observations.

In conclusion, while we cannot say what part the Blackfoot played in the development of the material culture of the area we have shown their position in it both with reference to their immediate neighbors and the tribes of the whole.   While no one can say what the future will bring forth, we despair of ever reaching a more definite conclusion in their case.   It would seem that on the whole from the standpoint of material culture, in this area the traditional linguistic units have little weight, the linguistic factor being almost negligible in the face of geographical continuity and economic uniformity, suggesting that the ultimate method must be an intensive study of the distribution of a number of cultural traits for a considerable area.

BIBLIOGRAPHY.

ALLEN, J. A.   The American Bison, Living and Extinct. (Memoirs, Geological Survey of Kentucky, Vol. 1, Part 2).

BATTEY, THOMAS C.   Life and Adventures of a Quaker among the Indians. New York, 1876.

BRACKENRIDGE, H. M.   Journal of a Voyage up the River Missouri: performed in Eighteen Hundred and Eleven. Baltimore, 1816.

BRYCE, REV. GEORGE.   Remarkable History of the Hudson's Bay Company, including that of the French traders of Northwestern Canada and of the North-west and Astor Fur Companies. New York, 1900.

CARVER, J.   Travels through the Interior Parts of North America, in the Years 1766, 1767, and 1768. London, 1778.

CATLIN, GEO.   Illustrations of the Manners, Customs, and Conditions of the North American Indians. London, 1848.

CHAMBERLAIN, ALEXANDER F.   The Kootenay Indians. (Annual Archaeological Report, 1905. Appendix, Report, Minister of Education, p. 178. Toronto, 1906).

CLARK, W. P.   The Indian Sign Language. Philadelphia, 1885.

CURTIS, EDWARD S.   The North American Indian, 1909.

DENSMORE, FRANCES.   Plea of our Brown Brother and Ke-wa-kun-ah, the homeward way. Redwing, 1906.

DE SMET, FATHER.   Life, Letters and Travels of Father Pierre Jean De Smet, S. J. 1801–1873. Edited by Chittenden and Richardson. New York, 1905.

DORSEY, GEORGE A.   Traditions of the Skidi Pawnee. (Memoirs, American Folk-Lore Society, 1904, Vol. 8).

DORSEY, JAMES OWEN.   Omaha Dwellings, Furniture and Implements. (Thirteenth Annual Report, Bureau of American Ethnology, 1891–92, Washington, 1896).

EARLY WESTERN TRAVELS.   See Reuben Gold Thwaites.

FARRAND, LIVINGSTON.   Basis of American History, 1500–1900. The American Nation: a History, Vol. 2. New York, 1904.

FRANKLIN, JOHN.   Narrative of a Journey to the Shores of the Polar Sea. Philadelphia, 1824.

GREGG, JOSIAH.   Commerce of the Prairies. New York, 1845.

GRINNELL, GEORGE BIRD.   (a) Blackfoot Lodge Tales. New York, 1904.
(b) Pawnee Hero Stories and Folk-Tales. New York, 1893.
(c) The Story of the Indian. New York, 1904.
(d) Early Blackfoot History. (The American Anthropologist, Vol. 5, No. 2, April, 1892).
(e) The Lodges of the Blackfoot (American Anthropologist, N. S., Vol. 3).

GODDARD, PLINY EARLE. Life and Culture of the Hupa. (Publications of the University of California, pp. 88, Plates 30, September, 1903).

HALE, HORATIO. Report on the Blackfoot Tribes. (Report of the British Association for the Advancement of Science, September, 1885). London, 1886.

HAMILTON, W. T. My Sixty Years on the Plains, trapping, trading and Indian fighting. New York, 1905.

HANDBOOK OF AMERICAN INDIANS NORTH OF MEXICO. (Bulletin 30, Part 1, Bureau of American Ethnology, Washington, 1907).

HARMON, DANIEL W. A Journal of Voyages and Travels in the Interior of North America. New York, 1903.

HAYDEN, F. V. Contributions to the Ethnography and Philology of the Indian Tribes of the Missouri Valley. (Transactions, American Philosophical Society, Vol. 12, Article 3, Page 231. Philadelphia, 1863).

HECKEWELDER, REV. JOHN. Indian Nations. Philadelphia, 1876.

HECTOR AND VAUX. Notice of the Indians seen by the Exploring Expedition under the Command of Captain Palliser. By James Hector, M. D. and W. S. W. Vaux, M. A. (Transactions of the Ethnological Society of London, Vol. 1, London, 1860).

HENRY, ALEXANDER. Travels and Adventures in Canada and the Indian Territories, between the years 1760 and 1776. New York, 1809.

HENRY AND THOMPSON. New Light on the Early History of the Great Northwest. Edited by Elliott Coues. New York, 1897.

HILL-TOUT, C. The Native Races of the British Empire. North America. London, 1907.

HIND, HENRY YOULE. Narrative of the Canadian Red River Exploring Expedition of 1857 and of the Assiniboine and Saskatchewan Exploring Expedition of 1858. London, 1860.

HORNADAY, WILLIAM T. The Extermination of the American Bison, with a sketch of its Discovery and Life History. (Smithsonian Report, United States National Museum for 1887, Washington, 1889, pp. 367–548).

JAMES, EDWIN. Account of an Expedition from Pittsburgh to the Rocky Mountains, performed in the Years 1819, 1820. London, 1823.

KEATING, WILLIAM H. Narrative of an Expedition to the Source of St. Peter's River, Lake Winnepeck, Lake of the woods, &c., &c, performed in the year 1823. Philadelphia, 1824.

KROEBER, ALFRED L. (a) Ethnology of the Gros Ventre. (Anthropological Papers, American Museum of Natural History, 1908, Vol. 1, Part 4, pp. 141–282).

(b) The Arapaho. (Bulletin, American Museum of Natural History, New York, Vol. 18).

LARPENTEUR, CHARLES. Forty Years a Fur Trader on the Upper Missouri. Edited with notes by Elliott Coues. 2 volumes. New York, 1898.

LEWIS, ALBERT BUELL. Tribes of the Columbia Valley and the Coast of Washington and Oregon. (Memoirs of the American Anthropological Association, Vol. 1, Part 2. Lancaster, Pa., 1906).

LEWIS AND CLARK. Original Journals of the Lewis and Clark Expedition. (Thwaites Edition). New York, 1904.

MACLEAN, REV. JOHN. (a) The Mortuary Customs of the Blackfoot Indians. (Proceedings, Canadian Institute, Toronto, Third Series, Volume 5, 1886–87, Toronto, 1888).

(b) The Blackfoot Sun Dance. (Proceedings, Canadian Institute, Toronto, Third Series, Volume 6, 1887–88. Toronto, 1889).

(c) The Blackfoot Confederacy. (Proceedings, Canadian Institute, Toronto, Third Series, Volume 7, 1888–89. Toronto, 1890).

(d) Social Organization of the Blackfoot Indians. (Transactions, Canadian Institute, Volume 4, 1892–93. Toronto, 1895).

(e) The Gesture Language of the Blackfeet. (Transactions, Canadian Institute, Volume 5. Toronto, 1898).

(f) Picture-Writing of the Blackfeet. (Transactions, Canadian Institute, Volume 5. Toronto, 1898).

(g) The Blackfoot Language. (Transactions, Canadian Institute Volume 5. Toronto, 1898).

(h) Indians of Canada, Their Manners and Customs, Toronto 1907.

(i) Canadian Savage Folk. The Native Tribes of Canada. Toronto, 1896.

McCLINTOCK, WALTER. Medizinal-und Nutzpflanzen der Schwarzfuss-Indianer. (Zeitschrift für Ethnologie, Vol. 2, 1909.)

MARCY, RANDOLPH B. Explorations of the Red River of Louisiana, in the year 1852. Washington, 1854.

MASON, OTIS T (a) The Origins of Invention: a Study of Industry among Primitive Peoples. London, 1895.

(b) Cradles of the American Aborigines. (Smithsonian Report, United States National Museum for 1887, Part 2, Washington, 1889).

(c) Aboriginal American Basketry. Studies in a Textile Art without Machinery. (Smithsonian Report, United States National Museum for 1902, Washington, 1904).

(d) North American Bows, Arrows and Quivers. (Smithsonian Report, United States National Museum for 1893, Washington, 1894).

(e) Aboriginal Skin-Dressing. (Smithsonian Report, United States National Museum for 1889, Washington, 1891).

MATTHEWS, WASHINGTON. Ethnography and Philology of the Hidatsa Indians. (United States Geological and Geographical Survey, Miscellaneous Publications, No. 7. Washington, 1877).

MAXIMILIAN, PRINCE OF WIED. Travels in the Interior of North America. Translated by H. Evans Lloyd. London, 1843.

McDOUGALL, JOHN. Saddle, Sled and Snowshoe. Toronto, 1896.

MOONEY, JAMES. The Cheyenne Indians. (Memoirs, American Anthropological Association, Vol. 1, Part 6, pp. 357–642. Lancaster, Pa., 1907).

MORICE, REV. A. G. (a) The Canadian Denes. (Annual Archaeological Report. 1905. Appendix, Report, Minister of Education, Toronto, 1906).

(b) The Western Denes. (Proceedings, Canadian Institute, Toronto, Third Series, Volume 7, 1888–89. Toronto, 1890).

(c) Notes on the Western Denes. (Transactions, Canadian Institute, Volume 4, 1892–93. Toronto, 1895).

MORSE, E. S. Ancient and Modern Methods of Arrow Release. (Bulletin of the Essex Institute, Vol. 17, 1885. Salem, 1886).

NELSON, EDWARD WILLIAM. The Eskimo about Bering Strait. (Eighteenth Annual Report, Bureau of American Ethnology, Part 1, Washington, 1897).

NUTTALL, THOMAS. A Journal of Travels into the Arkansas Territory during the year 1819. Philadelphia, 1821.

PALMER, DR. EDWARD. Food Products of the North American Indians. (Report, Commissioner of Agriculture, 1870, Washington, 1871).

PARKMAN, FRANCIS. (a) La Salle and the Discovery of the Great West. Boston, 1881.

(b) The Oregon Trail. Boston, 1881.

PIKE, CAPT. Z. M. An Account of Expeditions to the Sources of the Mississippi, and through the Western Parts of Louisiana, to the sources of the Arkansaw, Kans, La Platte, and Pierre Jaun Rivers; performed by orders of the Government of the United States during the years 1805, 1806, and 1807. Philadelphia, 1810.

RIGGS, STEPHEN R. Forty Years with the Sioux. Boston, 1880.

ROTH, H. LING. Moccasins and their Quill Work. (The Journal of the Royal Anthropological Institute of Great Britain and Ireland, Vol. 37. London, 1908).

RUSSELL, FRANK. Explorations in the Far North. (University of Iowa. 1898).

SCHOOLCRAFT, HENRY R. (a) Narrative Journal of Travels through the Northwestern Regions of the United States extending from Detroit through the Great Chain of American Lakes, to the Sources of the Mississippi River. Performed as a Member of the Expedition under Governor Cass. In the Year 1820. Albany, 1821.

(b) Historical and Statistical Information respecting the
History, Condition and Prospects of the Indian
Tribes of the United States. Philadelphia, 1851–
57.

SCHULTZ, J. W. My life as an Indian. New York, 1907.

SCOTT, H. L. The Early History and the Names of the Arapaho. (The American
Anthropologist, N. S., Vol. 9, 1907).

SPINDEN, H. J. (a) See G. F. Will.

(b) The Nez Perce Indians. (Memoirs of the American Anthropological Association, Vol. 2, Part 3).

SWAN, JAMES G. The Northwest Coast; or, Three Years in Washington Territory.
New York, 1857.

TEIT, JAMES. The Thompson Indians of British Columbia. (Memoirs, American
Museum of Natural History, Vol. 2, Part 4.
New York, 1900).

THWAITES, REUBEN GOLD. Early Western Travels, 1748–1846; a series of anno-
tated reprints of some of the best and rarest
contemporary volumes of travel, etc. Edited
with notes, introduction, index, etc. Cleveland,
1906.

TURNER, LUCIEN M. Ethnology of the Ungava District, Hudson Bay Territory.
(Eleventh Annual Report, Bureau of American
Ethnology, Washington, 1890).

TYLOR, EDWARD B. Researches into the Early History of Mankind and the Development of Civilization. New York. (No date.)

UMFREVILLE, EDWARD. Present State of Hudson's Bay and the fur trade. London,
1790.

WHIPPLE, LIEUT. A. W., THOMAS EWBANK, ESQ. AND PROF. WM. W. TURNER.
Report upon the Indian Tribes. (Reports,
Explorations and Surveys, 1853–4, Vol. 3, Part 3.
Washington, 1855).

WILL, G. F., AND H. J. SPINDEN. The Mandans: a study of their culture, archaeol-
ogy and language. (Papers, Peabody Museum,
Vol. 3, No. 4, Cambridge, 1906).

WILLOUGHBY, CHARLES C. Houses and Gardens of the New England Indians (The
American Anthropologist, N. S., 1906).

WISSLER, CLARK. (a) The Blackfoot Indians. (Annual Archaeological Report,
1905. Appendix, Report, Minister of Education.
Toronto, 1906).

(b) Decorative Art of the Sioux Indians. (Bulletin, American
Museum of Natural History, Vol. 18. New
York, 1904).

(c) Ethnographical Problems of the Missouri-Saskatchewan
Area. (American Anthropologist, Vol. 10, No. 2.)

(d) The Diffusion of Culture in the Plains of North America
(Proceedings of the Americanist Congress, Que-
bec, 1906.)

(e) Types of Dwellings and their Distribution in Central North
America. (Verhandlungen des xvi. Interna-
tionalen Amerikanisten-Kongresses.)